Reader's Digest
Household
Cleaning
Manual

Reader's Digest
Household
Cleaning
Manual

Cleaning tips, tricks and advice for every room in your home

Published by
The Reader's Digest Association Limited
London • New York • Sydney • Montreal

Contents

A new approach to cleaning

This book covers the full spectrum of topics related to cleaning – from smart routines and the right gear to handling unexpected messes and cleaning specific types of items and materials. But underlying it all is one key idea: the more you know about how to clean and the more organised you are about cleaning – the less effort, time and money you will have to spend actually doing it. Too many people see cleaning as an odious chore that can't be avoided, but is all too easy to put off. We're here to convince you of the opposite: that if you have a positive attitude to cleaning and its benefits, then a pristine house becomes something that is much easier to accomplish.

Ten golden rules of cleaning

Your primary goal in cleaning is to remove dirt, whether it be in your home or on your garments. But you do need to determine how far you are prepared to go. You don't want to injure yourself or damage the very thing you are trying to clean. And you also want to get it done as quickly and with as little effort as possible. Stick to the following ten golden rules and you will achieve safe, effective cleaning that attacks the problem early and with the minimum amount of effort.

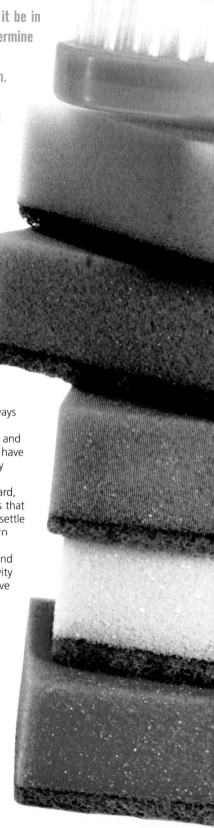

1 Clean up immediately Spills and stains are generally much easier to clean up when you deal with them immediately. When you treat the tomato sauce stain on your shirt at once, by rinsing it under the cold tap, it will offer little resistance. If you wait until the next day, you will expend a lot more cleaning solution and time getting rid of it. As a rough rule practically all clothing or carpet stains are easiest to remove when they are fresh. The longer you wait, the more chance the stain has to set. The rare exception is mud tracked onto your carpet. This is easiest to clean when you have let it dry first. So force yourself to hold back until it's bone dry and crumbly; then just vacuum it up.

2 Clean from the top down Don't fight gravity when you clean. You will lose. Working down from high to low almost always works better in cleaning situations.

When you are cleaning the entire house, start on the top floor and work your way down to avoid tramping dirt through rooms you have already cleaned. When you are cleaning a room, first remove any cobwebs from the ceiling and coving. Then dust light fixtures, followed by window frames and wall hangings. Moving downward, sweep over the furniture, skirting boards and floors. This ensures that any dust shaken loose from higher up does not float down and settle on something you have already cleaned below. You don't want to have to dust the room twice.

Similarly, when you clean windows and mirrors, start up high and work your way down, because your cleaning solution obeys gravity and may drip down over previously cleaned surfaces. This will save you both elbow grease and time.

3 Think dry, then wet When you are cleaning a room, start with the cleaning jobs that require dry methods (dusting, sweeping, and vacuuming, for instance). If you still need to clean, then move on to wet methods, using an all-purpose cleaner and glass cleaner, mopping and similar jobs. This way, there will be less dirt floating around in the room to cling to wet surfaces.

4 Start with the least harmful approach Use your gentlest cleaning methods first and move up to more aggressive techniques only if necessary. If you have tried everything you know to be safe, make a rational decision about whether it's worth carrying on. Generally, you may feel it is better to suffer a small spot on your hob, than to ruin the surface by scrubbing it with steel wool.

5 **Let time do the work for you** Here's a little time management trick to make your cleaning easier and faster. When you start to clean a room, spray on your cleaning chemicals first and then find another little job to do while the cleaner does its dirty work. In the kitchen, spray your cleaner on the worktops and appliances, then occupy yourself with removing old food from the fridge while the cleaner soaks in. When you come back to wipe clean, there should be little or no scrubbing to do.

6 **Carry your supplies with you** Keep your core cleaning products with you. This will save you from making multiple trips around the house looking for the right tools and cleaners.
Use one of the following to carry your tools:
• A simple plastic tool caddy from a DIY store – the sort painters use – with two deep pockets each side of a handle, is perfect.
• A sturdy, large plastic bucket with a good handle.
• An apron with roomy pockets.
As well as cleaning solutions and cloths, put in clean rags, paper towels, and a stack of bin liners for emptying all of the wastebaskets around the house. If your home has more than one floor, consider setting up a caddy for each level. However, only do this if you have somewhere safe, away from children, to store cleaning products safely.
If you have room and secure space in the toilet and bathroom, you might prefer to leave speciality cleaning products here, rather than carry them around with you.

7 **When in doubt, test it out** Before you use a new cleaning technique or product, test the method on an inconspicuous area of the object you are cleaning. This rule also applies when you first clean an object that is delicate and might be damaged by a cleaning compound. Testing will show you whether the object is colourfast and whether the cleaning method is likely to cause damage.

8 **Don't soak, go easy on the spray** When you clean an item that could be harmed by a liquid cleaning product – electronics, computer screens, framed artwork, or framed photographs, for example – first spray the cleaner on your cleaning cloth and then wipe. Don't spray cleaner directly on the object you are cleaning. Liquid slopping into your electronics could cause serious damage, and solution dripping through a frame and soaking the matting could harm your artwork.

9 **Read the directions** You have probably heard this before. But the makers of all of the furnishings in your home do know best how to clean them. And the manufacturers of your cleaning products know the best way to use them. So where possible, follow the manufacturer's directions when cleaning anything. This goes for everything from toasters to silk blouses. File the directions and cleaning tips that come with any new appliance, rug or other household item and keep them. Unlike guarantees, cleaning instructions are valid for as long as you have the item. Don't remove care labels on clothes, linens and other washable objects – they are there to help you.

10 **Get some protection** Last but not least, take care of yourself. Many cleaning products contain acid, bleach, abrasives and other ingredients that can damage eyes, skin, nose, and even lungs. Don't let your cleaning products get mixed together. Some combinations – chlorine bleach and ammonia, for instance – will produce poisonous gases. When you are using cleaning chemicals, make sure the room is properly ventilated.

Blitz the house in a morning

Here is a foolproof system for completing all your weekly house cleaning, from top to bottom, as swiftly and efficiently as possible. you will whip through regular chores, spending less time yet getting better results. Read on and discover how simple it is. Professional housekeepers say you need just two things to do a speedy but thorough job of cleaning your home: focus and organisation.

Assemble your arsenal

An effective cleaning system starts with good tools and products.

Use a plastic or rubber cleaning caddy with dividers, stocked with everything you will need as you make your rounds. Check your tools regularly to make sure they are up to the task: A crumbling sponge mop or worn-out broom will make extra work. A vacuum cleaner with a broken guard will damage skirtings and furniture.

For a house with several floors, it's worth keeping a completely stocked cleaning caddy on each floor, providing that you have somewhere safe to store chemicals out of children's reach. Also keep basic tools, including a broom, dustpan and mop, on every level.

Alternatives to the caddy, especially if you have a smaller house or flat, are a large plastic bucket, or an apron with large pockets. Arrange items in the caddy so that it is well balanced. Avoid specialised items that accomplish only one job, such as soap scum cleaner or special counter spray. If you must have such cleaners, store them near the place that you are most likely to need them.

Fill your caddy with these items:

Glass cleaner

General-purpose cleaner Choose one in a spray bottle – supermarket own-labels are good.

Heavy-duty degreasing cleaner Or a mousse product, like Cif, which is fast to use.

Wood polish

Powdered scouring cleanser such as Astonish or Bar Keeper's Friend. You will also need a few extra tools Some of these items may not be mentioned in the weekly routine described below, but you will need them for some of the cleaning jobs you will be doing:

Lambswool duster

Nylon scrubbing pad

Stiff-bristled toothbrush for scrubbing around taps.

1cm soft-bristled paintbrush for dusting lampshades and removing cobwebs.

Toilet bowl brush

Rubber gloves

Clean cotton rags

Micro fibre cloth (E-cloth)

Large rubbish bag

Plastic squeegee for bathrooms.

Safety glasses to protect your eyes from splattering cleaner or airborne dirt.

Plastic bin for collecting items that belong elsewhere.

Before you begin

Before we get down to the specifics of the household blitz, it's worth setting out some time-saving ground rules.

Clean from left to right and top to bottom
A systematic, clockwise approach to a room eliminates any retracing of steps. And a top-to-bottom system lets gravity work for you and avoids duplication of effort. Dust from window ledges won't fall onto a freshly cleaned table, for instance.

Keep cleaning supplies together and close at hand Interrupting the bathroom cleaning to track down window cleaner slows your momentum.

Deal with clutter separately The plan is about cleaning, not decluttering. So there should be no clothes strewn about the bedroom and no dishes left in the sink.

Move furniture toward the centre of the room when it is time to dust. The dust from the skirting board, carpets and windowsills will settle to the floor, where it's easy to vacuum up. Once you have vacuumed the outside of the room, push furniture into place and vacuum the rest.

Set a deadline Knowing up-front how much time you will spend cleaning can make the list of chores less daunting.

Learn to multitask If you must answer the phone, clean windows, polish a table or load the dishwasher at the same time.

Don't turn on the television Instead, use upbeat music to keep energised.

Use both hands Dust or wipe surfaces with one hand while lifting objects with the other. Scrub counters with a cloth in each hand. Squirt spray cleaner with one hand and wipe the surface with the other.

Pull a clean cotton tube sock over your dusting hand and lift objects with the other hand as you clean. If you have problems with dexterity, try a rubber glove on the hand you use for lifting objects.

Spray a lint-free towel with window cleaner and keep it handy for cabinets or tables with glass inlays.

If you have pets, use rubber gloves and a circular motion to collect pet hair from chairs and couches. Throw the rolled-up hair on the floor and suction it up when you vacuum the floor later.

If you live in a multistorey house and find items that belong elsewhere, place them in a plastic bin near the stairs and take them up next time you make the trip.

Get a 6-metre extension cord for your vacuum cleaner so you won't have to plug it in in every room.

If it's truly not dirty, don't clean it Don't waste time on a rarely-used room. Dust lightly and forget it.

The household blitz

The household blitz divides your home into four zones. You completely clean each zone before moving on to the next. You do not go over the same ground, or cleaning surface, twice, make extra trips around the house or counterproductive moves like wiping dust onto a just vacuumed floor.

Here are the four zones:

Zone 1 Bedrooms, bathroom and halls.
Zone 2 Kitchen, informal dining area and family room.
Zone 3 Formal living room and formal dining room.
Zone 4 Laundry room, home office and other miscellaneous spaces.

A lot of people have no idea how to clean and may typically start with the room nearest to where they store the vacuum cleaner. But professional cleaners work in a specific and organised way. And now you can too. With this system, you have an efficient step-by-step process that couldn't be easier to follow.

Zone 1: Bathroom Bedrooms & hall

Start with the areas which need the most 'laundry' doing: the bedrooms and bathroom. Gathering bedding and used towels into the washing machine will get everything moving quickly.

1 Go into each bedroom, strip the sheets off the beds, and throw them into the hall. Go into the bathroom and throw towels, washcloths and bath mats into the hall, too. Gather all of these washable items in a laundry basket and put them near the washing machine. Start a wash load with the bath mats and a couple of towels.

2 Get the upstairs cleaning caddy and go into the upstairs bathroom and start spreading around the cleaning chemicals. Spray cleaner inside the toilet bowl. Spray all-purpose cleaner or bathroom mousse, if you prefer, on the basin and basin surround and bath.

3 Empty the rubbish bin into the plastic bag that's in your cleaning caddy.

4 Now for some cleaning. Spray a clean rag with window cleaner and clean the mirror. Scrub the inside of your toilet bowl with the toilet bowl brush, then flush. Wipe down the basin, bath and surrounds. Rinse basins and baths. Spray all-purpose cleaner on the toilet seat and exterior and on the shower walls. Wipe everything down. (Note: this prevents mixing two cleaners in the toilet, which you must avoid.)

5 Mop the floor, backing out of the room.

6 Go into a bedroom and empty the rubbish basket into your plastic bag.

7 Move any light furniture or other obstructions toward the centre of the room, away from the walls.

8 Dust the entire room, starting at the entrance and moving from left to right (clockwise). Using your lambswool duster, take one wall at a time, working from top to bottom, including pelmets, window frames, pictures and furniture. Because your duster is on a pole, this isn't the arduous bending and stretching work it might sound.

9 Now vacuum around the entire outside of the bedroom. (That's why you moved the furniture.) Return the furniture to its original position. Starting at the far corner of the room, vacuum the rest of the room, backing out the door.

10 Go into the other upstairs bedrooms and repeat steps 6 to 9.

11 Give the upstairs hall a quick dusting, moving left to right, top to bottom, one wall at a time. Dust the tops of pictures and any skirtings.

12 Put away the upstairs cleaning caddy. Vacuum the upstairs hall, moving backwards toward the stairs. Take the rubbish bag with you and back down the stairs, vacuuming as you go.

13 Dust and vacuum the downstairs hallway.

14 Unload the washing machine – it should be finished by now. Put everything but the rubber bath mats into the tumble-dryer (if you have one – otherwise hang it up to dry with the bath mats). Load the machine with dirty sheets and towels. Hang the bath mats on a clothes rack or peg on the line to drip dry.

Zone 2: Kitchen, dining area and family room

You already have some of the biggest cleaning jobs behind you. Now it's time to tackle the real high-traffic spots: kitchen, casual dining area and the family room.

1 Get your downstairs cleaning caddy. Go into the kitchen and pull out a microwave-safe bowl. Pour in 2 cups of water, put the bowl of water in the microwave, and heat on high for 3 to 5 minutes.

2 While the microwave is running, go around the kitchen and wipe all surfaces, left to right, top to bottom. Spray on a cleaner that's safe for your hob (make sure

it's cool first), then also spray an appropriate kitchen cleaner onto the oven and refrigerator doors, and the worktops. If in doubt, the safest solution is sudsy water, made with warm water and washing-up liquid. Pour it into an empty plastic spray bottle. Then you are ready to go.

3 Take a cleaning cloth and move from left to right around the kitchen, wiping down the work surfaces and appliances. While you are at the stove, wipe any food spills from the cooking rings. Move worktop appliances such as the toaster and kettle and wipe under them as you go. When you get to the microwave, make sure the water has cooled for at least a minute. Pour the water out and wipe down the steamed interior of the microwave.

4 Pick one section of cabinets to clean each time you clean the kitchen. Spray that section with all-purpose spray and wipe. Each month or so, you will have worked right round the room with no need to ever make cleaning cupboard doors a separate major cleaning job.

5 Throw out old food in the refrigerator and pick one shelf or drawer to clean. At the sink, carefully wash it with sudsy water. Then rinse very thoroughly. Dry glass shelving carefully using a fresh, lint free linen tea-towel.

6 Clean the sink. Stainless steel can scratch, so you should avoid using anything abrasive. A light scouring cream like Cif is generally suitable. But if in doubt, simply use a cloth and washing-up liquid. Shiny taps are the trademark that a professional cleaner's been in – use a microfibre cloth to dry them, and you will get a polished look in no time.

7 Mop the floor.

8 Go to your casual dining area. (If you have an eat-in kitchen, take care of the table and chairs in step 3.) Dust your way around the room, left to right, top to bottom. Dust the light fixture. Pull the chairs away from the table. Wipe up any spills or crumbs from the table and chairs. Mop or vacuum under the table and move the chairs back. Clean the rest of the floor.

9 Go to your family room. Move any light furniture into the centre of the room. Move around the room dusting – from left to right, top to bottom, one section of wall at a time. Dust the pelmets, window frames, pictures, furniture and electronic devices.

10 Vacuum the outside of the family room. Put furniture back in its original position. Vacuum the rest of the room.

11 Take the towels, washcloths and bath mats out of the dryer or off the line and set them on a worktop. (Don't bother folding.) Take the sheets and towels out of the washing machine and put them in the dryer. Load any remaining sheets and towels in the washing machine.

Zone 3: Formal living and dining rooms

Take a deep breath, a drink of water and pat yourself on the back. You are almost done – and by following a clear cleaning system, you have left the easiest for last.

1 Go into your formal living room. Move any light furniture, including lamps, into the centre of the room.

2 You know the drill by now. Dust the room, moving from left to right, one wall at a time. Dust from top to bottom, including pelmets, window frames, pictures and furniture.

3 Vacuum the outside of the living room. Return the furniture to its original position.

4 Lift the seat cushions out of the sofa and armchairs and vacuum underneath with the brush attachment. Vacuum the centre of the floor.

5 Go to the dining room and repeat steps 1 to 3.

6 Dust the dining room table and chairs.

7 Pull the chairs away from the table and vacuum under the table. Return the chairs to their original positions and vacuum the rest of the room.

Zone 4: Laundry room and other spaces

This is the home stretch – it's time to polish off the last couple of rooms and wrap up any loose ends.

1 Remove the sheets and towels from the dryer or washing line and add them to the unfolded pile on the counter. Move the last of the laundry from the washer to the dryer or the washing line.

2 Empty the rubbish bin into a plastic bag.

3 Since this is not a high-traffic area, a quick dusting will do. Move around the room left to right, top to bottom, dusting the shelves, worktops and sink. Wipe up any detergent spills with a damp rag.

4 Mop the floor.

5 Continue the pattern of dusting and then vacuuming or mopping in the other miscellaneous spaces of your home – conservatory, enclosed porch and office.

6 Empy the vacuum cleaner cylinder (or check on the bag level) then put it and your cleaning caddy away.

7 Take your plastic bag full of rubbish out to the dustbin.

8 While you are outside, take your doormats and shake them out thoroughly, into an unobtrusive spot.

9 Take all your dirty cleaning cloths to the laundry room and put them in the washing machine.

10 Once all of the sheets, towels and other household laundry items are dry, spread out one of the sheets from an upstairs bedroom and put all of the other laundry on top of it, along with the bathroom mats that were drip-drying. Pull the corners of the sheet together to make a sack. Take it all to the first-floor bedrooms and put the sheets back on the beds. (This is why you didn't bother folding.) Return the towels, washcloths and bath mat to their usual places. Then carry the remaining laundry upstairs and repeat. Of course, if you have several sets of bedding and you like to rotate, you will need to fold the sheets up, then take fresh supplies from the airing cupboard.

11 Take a bow. Or take a nap – it's your choice and you are bound to have plenty of time, because the beauty of this system is how fast everything gets done.

General household cleaning

A number of items that you need to clean are found throughout the house: carpets and hard flooring; doors and wall-coverings, panelling and general woodwork and various kinds of glazing. The following section covers the most effective ways to clean these surfaces and fittings, covering both everyday maintenance and more vigorous techniques for dealing with stains or frequently neglected areas such as attics and basements.

Attics & lofts

Give the attic an annual clean and you will remove a source of dust, mould and other potentially hazardous substances from your home.

Wear a full mouth-nose dust mask, especially if you haven't ventured into the attic for a while, an apron to protect your clothes, goggles and heavy rubber gloves. If the attic is used for storage, make sure everything is organised beforehand by storing small items in labelled boxes, grouping together boxes that contain like items and creating paths so that you can get at any item.

To clean the attic use an extension lead, so that you can vacuum and suck up dust from the top down – ceiling, beams, walls and floor. Clean around and under stored items. Once the major grime has been dealt with, give the area a light once-over with a damp cleaning cloth dipped in a solution of water and washing-up liquid.

Knock down cobwebs with a long-handled broom, sweep the floor and brush away debris from the walls. In a bucket, mix hot water and an all-purpose cleaner. If the walls need cleaning, wash them first, using a strong-bristled floor brush with a long handle. Start at the bottom and work upwards. While standing in one spot, wash as much as you can reach, then rinse with warm water, from a second bucket.

Scrub concrete floors using hot water and household detergent. Because concrete is porous, strong odours can be hard to eradicate. If a hard scrub doesn't get rid of them, you can seal the floor with a concrete sealer, which is stronger than wax. Follow the label directions and spread it on with a mop. Repeat the application for really tough odours. After cleaning, open any doors or windows to air out the room and help the drying process.

If mould or mildew is a problem, take an extra step after cleaning. Mop the walls and floors with a solution of 100ml chlorine bleach to 15 litres of water, then rinse well. Keep in mind that the bleach will kill existing mildew, but it will return unless the source of the moisture is addressed.

Basements & cellars

Dealing with a dirty or recently flooded basement is a daunting cleaning task – but it can be done.

Make sure you are well protected with a dust mask and strong rubber gloves.

Banisters

A beautiful staircase and banister rail can be the centrepiece of a home's entrance, so don't let everyday grime diminish its impact.

Dust a painted banister with a soft, water-dampened cloth. If it is especially dirty, add a couple of drops of mild washing-up liquid to warm water Then wash and rinse a small section at a time, keeping the cloth well wrung out and wipe with a dry cloth. Oil polish is best avoided on painted wood, since it can discolour it. Wax is rarely needed, but if you use it, choose a light-coloured wax for light-coloured paint.

Dust a wooden banister with a soft cloth and furniture polish. That will restore moisture to the wood and keep the dust collected on the cloth from floating back onto the balusters (the posts or spindles that support the banister). When dust collects in intricate carvings on the balusters, use a cotton bud to get into crevices and clean out the tight spaces more thoroughly.

Carpets

For routine carpet cleaning, a vacuum cleaner is the best tool. Vacuuming removes about 85 per cent of carpet dirt. To get rid of deep-seated dirt, you will need to give carpets a more thorough cleaning. How often depends on your lifestyle – every 6 to 18 months is a reasonable estimate.

Vacuuming your carpet every day is ideal. Many people settle on once a week, even if it doesn't appear dirty. If you can, vacuum heavily trafficked areas a little more often. And be sure to vacuum up any obvious soiling before it gets ground in.

The more powerful your machine,the better. An upright vacuum has a brush bar to beat more dirt up out of the carpet. Or use a cylinder with a power nozzle, which relies on suction alone, but can come in handy if you lack the strength to push an upright, or find it awkward on stairs.

Vacuuming tips
• You may need to go over a piece of carpet up to seven times.
• Set the vacuum according to the pile level of the carpet – unless it has an automatic adjustment.
• Use slow, even strokes and go back and forth several times, to work both with and against the grain of the carpet pile. Finish with strokes that all go in the same direction. In plush carpets with pile, this will give a smooth finish, rather than just-cut lawn stripes.
• Move light furniture into the centre of the room before you start.
• If you have a rug, occasionally turn it over and vacuum the underside.
• If the vacuum cleaner won't suck up cat hairs, threads or other fine items, use a lint roller or a piece of doubled-over tape to pick them up.

Professional steam cleaning will remove ground in dirt from the carpet. The Rolls-Royce method is done by professionals using a truck-mounted unit. A good compromise is to shampoo the carpet, using a water-extraction machine. You can hire these from DIY stores and supermarkets for around £20 per day, with cleaning solutions for a typical home doubling your final cost. Or, you can buy your own machine from around £250.

Using a home-cleaning carpet shampooer
First vacuum the carpet. Move furniture out of the room, or to the sides. Follow the machine instructions on filling with shampoo and water: the best machines heat it to the correct temperature inside. Note that the water must be warm, not hot for wool based carpets, to avoid shrinkage.

Start in the far corner of the room, and move very slowly up and down. Move too quickly, and the machine will lay down wet shampoo solution, but won't have the time to suck it up. You will have to keep stopping to empty out dirty water and refill with shampoo and fresh water. When you have finished, open the windows to air the room. Wait until the carpet is quite dry before putting back heavy furniture or walking on it in shoes. Wet carpet is most vulnerable to damage.

Removing spots If your carpet is old and beaten up, you can afford to be daring in your treatment. If it's brand-new, of high quality and you want it to last for many years to come, be more cautious.

Stain removal techniques go from the most gentle and universal of cleaning substances – water – to far more extreme treatment. Be sure to blot, not rub, at the stains. Before moving from one step to the next, test the next solution on an inconspicuous area of carpet. Put a little of the treatment on the carpet, let it sit for about 10 minutes, and blot with a clean white rag. Inspect the rag for any dye from the carpet, and inspect the carpet for any damage. If a wool carpet doesn't respond to water and a mild soap solution, you should call a professional.

Here are the techniques to try, in order. Use one at a time, and always rinse well between steps.

1 Blot up liquid spills promptly then dilute what remains with water and blot some more. You can also dilute using plain mineral water.

2 Next, try a general-purpose spot cleaner. Mix 1 teaspoon of mild washing-up liquid with 100ml of warm water. Blot it on the spot. Rinse well with clean water.

3 Use a solution of 15ml of ammonia and 50ml of water on old spots, blood and chocolate.

4 Try 1 part white vinegar and 2 parts water on mildew stains and spills with a strong residual odour, such as urine.

5 Try full-strength 3 per cent hydrogen peroxide on tomato-based stains, red drinks, alcoholic drinks, fruit juice, grass stains, coffee and chocolate. Dab onto a cotton bud and press into the stain. Use a fresh cotton bud to lift off the solvent and the dissolved stain.

6 Use methylated spirits full strength, on oily stains, ballpoint pen ink, candle wax residue and grass stains. Use the cotton bud treatment, as above.

Special situations

• **For oily spills,** such as mayonnaise, salad dressing and butter, try saturating the spot with cornflour, a good absorbent. Allow it to dry, then vacuum.
• **For candle wax,** use a warm iron over a sheet of greaseproof paper to take up as much wax as possible. Then dab on methylated spirits. If there is still a stain, move on to the general-purpose spot cleaner described previously. (See step 2.)
• **For pet accidents** First, flush the spot with water and blot with an old towel or rag. Then use the general-purpose spot treatment. (See step 2, left.) Rinse that with the vinegar mixture. (See step 4.) Rinse again with water and blot. Apply a 1cm thick layer of dry, clean white rags, towels, or paper towels, weight them with a heavy object, and allow them to sit for several hours. If they're still damp when you remove them, repeat with a fresh layer of absorbent materials until they come up dry. The odour will not come out as long as any urine remains. So repeat until you are sure no smell remains.

If you have been removing spots, let the carpet dry first. Sprinkle bicarbonate of soda over the entire carpet, let it sit for three to five hours, and vacuum it up.

Chlorine bleach, iodine, mustard, insecticides and plant fertilisers, are likely to create permanent stains. Many foods, drinks, medicines and cosmetics stains may also be permanent.

As a last resort, take a pair of nail scissors and snip off the very worst of the stained pile. Then, leave a small ice cube to melt on the spot. The remaining fibres should swell a little to help plug the gap.

Ceilings

Ceilings attract airborne dirt, cigarette smoke and grease. Cleaning them is a project that's tempting to put off as they are hard to reach. Try to use long-handled tools instead of balancing on a ladder or step stool.

Dusting the ceiling is sometimes all that's needed. Use a long-handled duster. If you don't have one, simply tie a duster onto the end of a broom. Or you can suck, rather than sweep up dust, using your vacuum cleaner with a brush attachment.

To clean a very dirty ceiling you have to use water. Lay down dust sheets or newspapers to protect furniture, electronic equipment and floors. Wear safety goggles or other eye protection, because you are likely to dislodge small particles that you may not be able to see. You should also wear rubber gloves – wearing sweat bands designed for sport on your wrists will stop dirty water dripping up your arms.

To wash the ceiling, use a sponge mop with an extender handle. Be careful to apply even pressure and get an even distribution of the cleaning product so it won't streak. Or you can use a dry foam sponge, and stand on a stepladder. Break the ceiling into imaginary small squares and get off and move the stepladder each time you go to start a new 'square'.

For painted ceilings, whether they are covered with emulsion or gloss paint, a general-purpose cleaner, such as Flash, works well. Or use a concentrated one, like Zoflora, mixing both to packet instructions. Dip your sponge in the solution, wring out the excess and wipe the dirty area. Rinsing is necessary only if the ceiling is heavily soiled, but whether or not you rinse, you will need to wipe away the excess moisture with a dry towel to prevent bead marks.

Artex ceilings and those that have a rough surface are best kept dry. So keep running over it with the vacuum cleaner and the soft brush attachment.

Ceramic tiles

The beauty of ceramic tiles, besides their attractive appearance, is their durability and low maintenance. An alcohol-and-water solution is usually all that's needed to keep ceramic tiles shining, assuming that they were properly sealed during installation.

If you are not sure of this – perhaps with ageing, hand-fired tiles, play safe and use just a dampened sponge. You can then repaint the tiles, using a primer, then a top coat. On all kinds of tiles, over-harsh cleaners will do more damage than anything else, because they can strip away the protective sealant.

Cleaning ceramic tile floors regularly is important so that tracked-in dirt isn't able to build up and scratch through the protective sealant. Begin by removing loose dirt using a vacuum cleaner, a broom, or an

oil-free dust mop. Then add an all-purpose floor cleaner – a supermarket own label brand is fine. Avoid products that contain natural waxes – you don't want to slip up later. The waxes can penetrate into the grout (the substance in the seams between the tiles) and cause it to discolour.

Rinse twice with clean water to remove any chemicals that could break down the sealant. When the water rinses clean, dry the floor with a clean, soft cloth.

Clean ceramic wall tiles by wiping them down once or twice a month using all-purpose cleaner, or, if you are in the bathroom, the same bathroom cleaning mousse that you use on the sinks and bath. Areas such as the shower surround and the sink backsplash which collect soap scum and spatters, may need more frequent attention, especially in a large household.

Cleaning the grout between tiles is occasionally necessary. Mix together 30ml of vinegar with 3 litres of water and scrub the grout with a toothbrush or nylon scrubbing pad. Don't use steel wool, because it can scratch the finish.

Doormats

At some point, a doormat will have absorbed all the dirt it can take. Then it simply becomes a bridge over which dirt travels into your house.

First, knock out the dirt Go outside – well away from your house. Grab two adjacent corners of the doormat and shake hard. The loosest dirt will come off easily. Then, wearing goggles, drape the mat over a post or clothesline and use a heavy stick to beat it. After you have beaten out all the loose dirt, take a wire brush to dislodge the stubborn stuff. If wax or chewing gum is still clinging to the mat, press an ice cube against the offending lump until it's brittle enough to scrape off with a spoon.

To remove serious stains on a doormat made of rubber or rope, use an aerosol spot remover, such as Vanish. If you think it needs a more thorough cleaning, wash it in the washing machine on a gentle cycle.

If you have wooden doormats that are seriously stained you may need to strip off the existing coating, sand right down and then revarnish.

Doors & woodwork

Treat wooden doors in the same way as you would furniture made from the same material.

To remove surface dirt, dust with a dry towel. Tie a soft, old towel over the bristle end of a broom and brush into the angles and crevices. Use a toothbrush to get into tight corners or detailed moulding.

For stained wood, use soapy wood cleaner and mix with water according to the directions on the label.

For painted wood, all-purpose cleaner is the quickest and cheapest option.

Remove grease and surface dirt from paint using sugar soap. Using a sponge, start at the bottom, scrub in small circular motions. Rinse the sponge often and thoroughly to avoid putting dirt back on the door. Keep the solution clean and you won't have to rinse.

Drawers

Empty the drawer onto a table top covered with old newspaper. Then sort through and throw away everything you no longer want.

Next, clean the drawer
• **For wood,** use a little soapy wood cleaner, mixed according to directions or mix 1 litre warm water and 2 tablespoons of washing-up liquid in a large bowl.
• **For laminated plastic,** use 30ml of white vinegar in a litre of warm water.
• **For metal drawers,** put some bicarbonate of soda in a small bowl and add just enough water to make a paste.

Thoroughly soak a sponge and squeeze well, then wipe away at the drawer, inside and out. You can let the drawer air-dry, but if you are in a hurry to put your bits away again – only the must-keep stuff – dry it with a paper towel.

Dust

More than 5000 different materials, including skin flakes, pet hair, human hair, food bits, pollen grains, spores, insect parts, sawdust and clothing fibres combine to make the dust that settles on every surface in our homes.

Many methods of dusting simply push dust around. Feather dusters are great, for instance, for cleaning blinds – as long as you make sure to shake the duster outside frequently. But basically, a dry dust cloth just moves the dust or suspends it. But if you use a just-damp duster the dust will cling to your cloth and disappear for ever when you wash it in the washing machine.

To dust a room and cut down on the time dusting takes, vacuum everything first – furniture, walls, windowsills, upholstery, the coffee table. Vacuuming removes a lot of dust without creating a dust storm in the process. Follow up with a damp cloth and your room should be dust-free for a while.
   Microfibre cloths are great at holding onto the dust, because they have so many extra fibres. Generally, a little water on your just-damp dust cloth is all it takes. But if you have to deal with a great deal of grease, you will move faster if you spray on a dot of multi-purpose surface cleaner, provided that you just use it on the hard surfaces of your home that are listed as 'safe' on the cautions panel of your cleaner.

Floors

Even among general categories such as wood, stone or tile floors, there are vast differences between specific examples.

General guidelines for floor cleaning:
• Vacuum or sweep up loose dirt frequently.
• Use a dust mop – or tie a duster onto the base of a broom – to remove dust and cobwebs from corners.
• Wipe up any spills immediately.
• Clean with a damp mop or cloth (using plain water) weekly or more often. Change the water as soon as it gets cloudy.
• Use stronger cleaners only when a damp mop won't do the job.
• Rinse thoroughly after using any kind of cleaner.

To clean stone flooring, sprinkle damp sawdust over the floor, scrub with a stiff brush and sweep up the sawdust with a broom and dustpan. Then vacuum.
   Many kinds of stone flooring, especially marble, need a neutral pH cleaner (sold by businesses that sell and install stone flooring). A mild washing-up liquid mixed with water will also work nicely. Consult the dealer who sold you the stone for recommendations for specific cleaners if more power is needed. There are also professionals who can refinish stone floors.

To clean ceramic tile floors, a quick once-over with a damp mop is often all that is needed.
   When damp mopping isn't enough, mix a capful of methylated spirits in 4 litres of water. Apply the solution with a mop or an electric cleaner-polisher. Rinse well with clear water on your mop. A commercial cleaner such as Microshield Floor Tile Cleaner has the added benefit of containing an anti-mould ingredient which is handy if your floor is prone to dampness.
   If the grout needs attention, mix 50ml vinegar with 4 litres water and scrub with a toothbrush or nylon scrubbing pad. For heavy-duty treatment, scrub with a mixture of 100ml of chlorine bleach in 2 litres of water (wear rubber gloves). Let the solution stand for 20 minutes, mop the floor twice with clean water to rinse thoroughly and wipe dry. To make future cleaning easier, it's worth sealing the grout with a silicone sealer, available at home stores, hardware stores or specialist tile shops.

To clean wood floors you will have to get down on your hands and knees and use water sparingly.

When damp mopping isn't enough to shift grease or serious dirt, try one of these general-purpose cleaners:
• Mix 100ml cider vinegar in 4 litres of warm water.
• Brew some tea using 2 tea bags per 1 litre water. Dip a soft cloth or sponge in the solution, wring it out and wipe the floor. Then to finish, buff with a soft, dry cloth.

Determining a wood floor's finish will help you to work out how to care for it. If the floor was installed or last refinished before the mid 1960s, the finish is probably varnish or shellac. These finishes rest on top of the wood, are often waxed and require a whole-floor sanding before a new finish can be applied. Later finishes may be polyurethane, which penetrates the wood, should not be waxed and can be touched up by new urethane applied to the worn places. You can tell one from the other by scratching the surface with a coin in an inconspicuous place. If the finish flakes, it is probably shellac or varnish. If the finish does not flake, it is probably urethane.

To check for wax, put a couple of drops of water on the floor. Wait 10 minutes and check to see whether white spots have appeared under the water. White spots mean the floor has been waxed.

On varnished or shellacked floors, a solvent-based liquid wax for wood works well. It removes dirt and most of the old wax, prevents wax build-up and leaves a thin coating of new wax. You can apply the cleaner with a soft, dry cloth attached to a long-handled wax applicator, but you will do a better job on your hands and knees. You can also use an electric polisher, changing the pads frequently. In any case, you must buff afterward with a clean cloth. Never use water-based self-polishing wax on wood floors.

On urethane-finished floors, rub with a cloth containing a little furniture oil to give them more shine. (Read the label to make sure it doesn't contain any wax.) Be sure to use very little; too much oil will attract dirt – and turn the floor into a skating rink.

To clean vinyl flooring that just needs touching up, use a damp mop. If it is very diry, mix 250ml of white vinegar with 4 litres water and apply with a mop. Apply a small amount with your mop, then rinse thoroughly by mopping with plain water.

To add shine, apply a thin coat of wax to a dry, clean floor. The one-step wax-and-clean products don't work as well as a regular wax. A self-polishing wax is easy to apply, but it will build up over time. A solvent-based paste wax is more work and must be buffed but gives superior results.

No-wax vinyl has a polyurethane finish that is intended to keep a shine without waxing. It will stay shiny for a long time if it is kept clean, but eventually the finish will dull. Follow the manufacturer's instructions for using a polish or sealer to restore the shine. Use shampoo to remove hairspray build-up – a squirt of shampoo in 4 litres of water, then mop and rinse.

Clean marble floors with a gentle liquid soap that does not have a grease remover. The safest course is to take it easy. Mix about 2 tablespoons of mild liquid soap, Ivory, for instance, in 4 litres water. Using a soft sponge or a sponge mop if you are cleaning a marble floor, wipe the marble clean. Follow with two to three water rinses, depending on how soapy the cleaning mixture is. Dry with a soft cloth.

Clean marble floors regularly, before dirt and grit have a chance to scratch the surface. Wipe up spills immediately. As with a wood surface, avoid putting drinks glasses directly on marble, which can cause water rings. Water should bead on the marble. If the surface appears to be absorbing liquid, it's not sealed properly.

Reseal your marble floor annually at least – it's as easy as waxing a floor. Buy a stone sealer from a DIY store. Take a sponge, sponge mop or rag and cover the entire marble surface, including corners. There's no need to strip the floor before you seal.

To clean surface stains, use a marble polishing powder, such as tin oxide, which is available at DIY stores. Follow the product's directions to the letter. If the marble item you are cleaning is stained, but not of great value, you can try removing them with a thick paste made of baking soda and water. Apply the paste to the stain. Cover the paste with a sheet of plastic to keep the paste damp and let it sit for 10 to 15 minutes before wiping it off. Rinse with warm water and dry. Repeat the procedure if the first application doesn't fully remove the stain. If stains still remain, you will have to call on the expertise of a professional marble restorer.

To clean laminate flooring, keep in mind that, like wood, it should not be mopped by slopping lots of water around on the floor. (Laminate is the manmade flooring that comes in tongue-and-groove planks that often simulate wood.) Don't use ammonia, solvents, abrasives, general-purpose cleaners, polishes or waxes on laminate. Despite these restrictions, laminate is very easy to clean.
    If laminate gets scratched, you may be able to buy a touch-up stick from the manufacturer. With severe damage, you may be able to replace a plank or two – especially if you have laid the floor yourself and have a few off-cuts put by.

Painted surfaces

Paint is a decorative and protective coating. But even though it is made to stand up to much wear and tear, you must take care when cleaning it.

Strong chemical cleaners or too much scrubbing to remove greasy fingerprints can dull the paint's finish, creating an uneven patchiness that will clearly show up. In bad cases, over zealous cleaning can remove paint altogether. Since touch-up painting, even with a colour match, tends to look splotchy, a cleaning mistake could lead to a complete repainting, which is not what you want to happen.

Dust painted surfaces regularly, to keep dirt and grime from staining the surface when smeared or moistened. For painted furniture, shelves, door and window trim or knickknacks that are coated in a gloss paint, use a clean dust cloth, either dry or slightly dampened with water. Dusting – especially wet dusting – entire walls is not feasible, since many walls are covered with emulsion-based paint, which wet dusting could actually remove.

To remove stubborn stains from gloss paint, try wiping gently with a cloth dampened with a solution of warm water and washing-up liquid. If that doesn't work, try an all-purpose cleaner, but only after testing the cleaner on an inconspicuous corner of your painted surface. Clean from the bottom up so that your cleaning solution doesn't drip down, pick up grime and leave dirty streaks. Rinse with a clean, moist cloth or sponge. Dry well with clean towels to prevent water from damaging the paint or what's beneath it.

To remove marks from emulsion paint, first try rubbing with a white rubber, available from an office supply store for removing pencil marks. If that doesn't work, try gently wiping the marks with a water-moistened cloth. Blot dry soon afterward with a clean towel. Be careful: water can stain or remove emulsion paint.

Panelling

Panelling comes in two main varieties: real wood and simulated wood. Real wood panelling, made of walnut, oak, maple or other kinds of woods, is hardly different in quality from most wooden furniture. It is usually either sealed with a hard surface coat, such as varnish or polyurethane, or a stain or oil finish. Simulated wood is often coated in plastic. Understanding these differences is crucial when deciding how to clean panelling.

To remove dust from raised moulding, carving or other features, vacuum regularly using a brush attachment, or wipe with a cloth. For simulated wood, you can use a moistened dust cloth, but avoid using water on real wood. Moisture can damage wood.

To clean real wood with a surface coat, such as polyurethane, you may have to use water, but begin by trying a spray-on furniture polish, such as Pledge. These products remove dirt and dust while adding a hard wax finish. For heavier cleaning, try a cloth lightly dampened with a neutral cleaner, such as Pledge Soapy Cleaner.

To clean real wood with a penetrating finish, such as oil, use a cloth just dampened with methylated spirits, which will cut through the grease. Wipe gently back and forth in the direction of the wood grain. But work quickly and with care: methylated spirits will lift dirt and grime but will also remove the oil finish, so when you

have finished cleaning, you may well need to touch up – or reapply – the panelling's oil or stain finish. So only use this as last-resort cleaning. If you regularly wipe over with a just damp cloth, you should avoid needing to take this more drastic step.

Clean simulated wood panelling the same way you would a glossy painted surface. Its plastic coating, while not impermeable, means you can wipe it down with a cloth using a solution of warm water and a squirt of washing-up liquid. If you need something stronger, try an all-purpose cleaner, but only after testing the cleaner on an inconspicuous corner of the hardboard.

Rinse the hardboard panelling with a clean, moist cloth or sponge. Once the surface is clean, dry well with clean towels so that the water won't damage the compressed wood beneath the coating.

Radiators

Layers of dust can compromise the ability of a radiator to do its job and, because heat attracts dust, your radiator will be dustier than most other things in the room.

A weekly dusting with a feather duster or a dust cloth will keep accumulation down. Twice a year is often enough to do a major radiator cleaning, unless your environment is particularly dusty.

Remove as much of the surface dirt as possible using a hand vacuum or the brush attachment of your vacuum cleaner. The brush can actually go some way toward getting in between the tubes. But the thin nozzle attachment goes further. You won't get everything out with a vacuum, but there are more effective ways to clean inside the crevices.

To reach the dust trapped between tubes, use a couple of common kitchen items. Wrap a sheet of paper towel around the broad end of a kitchen spatula and secure it with a rubber band. Then slide the spatula up and down both sides of each tube of the radiator. For resistant substances and especially sticky spills, spray some all-purpose cleaner on the paper-swathed spatula and have another go at it.

Deal with rust spots as soon as you see them. You can get the larger chips off with a wire kitchen brush, followed by some medium and then fine-grade glasspaper. Be sure to get rid of all the rust so the corrosion will stop after painting. Once you have smoothed the surface and there is no visible rust residue, spray the spot with special radiator paint, available from DIY stores.

To clean a portable electric radiator, unplug it and then follow the directions given above for cleaning traditional steam radiators. (You won't need the de-rusting and painting steps.) When you put your electric radiator away for the summer, store it in a plastic rubbish bag so that it doesn't get dusty.

Shutters

Used to add character and cut down on strong sunlight and now often used as a smart alternative to blinds and curtains, shutters can become more unsightly than decorative if dust and grime accumulate.

Dust every month on both sides with the soft brush attachment of your vacuum. In between, touch up with a microfibre cloth or feather duster.

To clean indoor shutters, remove them from their hinges. Spray with a gentle all-purpose cleaner, taking special care to penetrate the cracks and crevices. Allow the cleaner to sit for five minutes. Wearing rubber gloves, start cleaning at the top and work toward the bottom. Clean the slats with a towel, your rubber-gloved fingers or a small soft-bristled brush for nooks and crannies. Use a trigger spray bottle filled with warm water to spray away dirt and other grime from the slats. Using a dry cloth, dry the slats one at a time. Reach hard-to-dry areas with a rag wrapped round the handle of a wooden spoon.

Cleaning outdoor shutters is basically the same operation – with a few refinements. Remove the shutters from the outside walls and lay them flat or prop them against a secure support. Wet down the shutters with an all-purpose cleaner or a spray bottle of water with a squirt of washing-up liquid added. Leave the cleaner on for a few minutes. Then use a screwdriver, wrapped in a towel, to attack hard-to-reach spots. Rinse with a garden hose, using as much water pressure as your hose can muster. Dry the slats with a towel. Let them finish drying in the sun.

Skylights

So you don't have to look up into a dirty sky, do some simple maintenance to preserve your view.

Clean the exterior of glass skylights using a long-handled squeegee. Use a commercial window cleaner that doesn't need rinsing or drying off.

A twice-a-year cleaning of skylights and their frames is sufficient; more often and you may wear out the silicone seal around the skylight and cause leaks.

The interiors of glass skylights can be cleaned monthly – or less if the skylight is difficult to reach. Wooden frames can be cleaned with a furniture polish if you can reach them. They'll also need to be finished, painted, or stained every three years to protect the wood against damage from ultraviolet rays.

If the skylight is made of acrylic, take care as strong cleaning solvents can easily scratch and damage the acrylic. Mix 1 tablespoon of washing-up liquid in 4 litres of warm water. Dip a soft cloth into the solution, wipe over the window and rinse well. If stubborn stains remain, use any plastic cleaner. Spray the cleaner on a cloth and wipe over the acrylic pane. You can also use the plastic cleaner to remove marks on vinyl frames.

If the skylight has a screen, you will need to remove it to clean the inside of the window. If this is too difficult, open the window and clean the inside at the same time that you clean the outside. To clean

the screen, vacuum it using the brush attachment. If the screen is really dirty and you can remove it, wash it with a soft brush dipped in a solution of washing-up liquid and warm water. Then rinse thoroughly.

Sliding doors

The sliding glass door to a patio or deck provides a beautiful view but can also collect a lot of sand, dust and debris in its tracks.

Vacuum the sill tracks at least once in spring and autumn, then weekly in summer. When you vacuum, pay extra attention to any carpet just in front of the door to help to reduce the amount of dirt that gets dragged into the tracks.

To keep the door sliding smoothly, spray silicone onto a soft, dry cloth and wipe it onto the track. Don't allow the silicone to come into contact with wood surfaces or the weather strip. Lubricate rollers with light oil such as 3-in-One.

To clean the outside of a vinyl frame, use a mild washing-up liquid solution – a couple of squirts to 3 litres of hot or warm water – and apply with a soft sponge or cloth. Rinse with clear water. Make sure to clean the frame before you wash the window. Start at the top of the frame and work down.

To clean the inside of a vinyl frame, wipe with a damp cloth when you clean the window. Don't use abrasive cleaners, scouring pads, or glasspaper to buff or remove marks – it will scratch the surface.

To clean wood-framed sliding doors, fill a misting bottle with warm water and a squirt of mild washing-up liquid. Lightly mist the sliding door frames and wipe off any dirt with a soft cloth. Finish by gently drying with another soft cloth. If stubborn grime won't come off with water or a mild detergent, consider sanding and refinishing.
  Make a thorough inspection of a wooden door frame at least once a year – more regularly if you live near the coast as wood is highly susceptible to attacks by fungi and other deterioration.

To clean aluminium-clad sliding doors, use washing-up liquid and water, applied with a sponge or soft brush from top to bottom. Rinse immediately. Air-dry or wipe with a soft, dry cloth. For a protective coating, apply car wax to the aluminium. All exterior aluminium frames should be cleaned annually.

Next, clean the glass, inside and out. (See Windows on page 29 for cleaning solutions and techniques.) Any window cleaner will be fine for this job, but avoid getting the cleaner on the window frames, because ingredients in some glass cleaners will damage the frame materials.

Vents

Set into floors, walls and ceilings, vents usually have angled louvres to keep large debris from getting into the house, whilst still allowing in air. They can be a real dust trap.

Vacuum the outside of the vent frequently. Make it part of your regular vacuuming routine, and you will cut down on dust and lint build-up considerably. Use a brush

attachment, which helps loosen dust. At least twice a year, remove registers and returns and clean both sides of them. Try cleaning them with the vacuum. If that does not completely remove the dust, wipe them with a moist dust cloth. If you replace filters behind your returns more often than twice a year, clean the return vents every time you remove them.

Wall coverings

The most common wall covering is washable wallpaper, treated with vinyl for easier cleaning. Other coverings include delicate papers, fabrics, grass, reeds, hemp, cork or leather. They are not usually washable, although some gentle cleaning methods won't hurt.

To determine whether wallpaper is washable, wet an inconspicuous area with a solution of a little washing-up liquid and water. If the paper absorbs water or darkens or if the colours run, it's not washable.

To clean washable wallpaper
• Don't flood the surface with water, over-wet the seams or edges or leave water on for more than a minute.
• Don't scrub unless the manufacturer says the covering can be scrubbed.
• Don't use harsh, abrasive cleaners.

To clean other wall coverings, vacuum regularly, using the small brush attachment. Some people also swear by using white bread. Simply ball up a slice until it is doughy in your hand, then roll it onto the dirty area. This should pick dirt up off the wallpaper. Keep going, with fresh pieces of bread, but making sure an already dirty surface never touches your wall.

Walls

How often walls need washing will depend largely on the hands and air that touch them. If you have a smoker or a wood-burning stove or fireplace in the house, your walls will show it. If you have children – they will add their own special touches to the walls.

To dust walls, use a lamb's wool duster or wrap a microfibre dust cloth or clean white cloth around a broom.

To remove spots, rub gently with a white art rubber or with a paste of bicarbonate of soda and water. Use white spirit on grease and WD-40 on crayon marks. Use methylated spirits on ink or marker spots.
  Apply cleaners to the cloth, not the wall and test on an inconspicuous area first.

Alcohol may remove paint from the wall if you are not careful. So try to work just along the stain line.

To wash down painted walls use:
• 200ml of ammonia, 1 teaspoon of washing-up liquid and 4 litres of water.
• Sugar Soap cleaner, made up as directed – on sale at DIY stores.
Keep the cleaning solution in one bucket and plain water for rinsing in another bucket. To protect the floor, use a dust sheet. To keep water from running down your arms when they are raised, wrap rags around your wrists and hold them on with rubber bands or elasticated hair ties.
  To clean the walls, wash with one of the solutions mentioned above using a natural sponge or a white cloth. Follow the guidelines below for applying the cleaning solution. Reach high points by standing on a sturdy stepladder that is tall enough so you won't need to stand on the upper two steps.

Start at the bottom; work your way up
Almost everywhere you clean, you are advised to start at the top and work down. However, some professional decorators start at the bottom and go up. The logic is that dirty water running down a dirty wall leaves worse streaks than dirty water running down a clean wall.

1 Apply cleaning solution over a small area at the bottom.

2 Wash, using circular strokes.

3 Rinse with plain water.

4 Dry with a towel.

5 Move up.

Windows

So much has been printed about the best way to clean windows that you might think it was an Olympic event. In fact, lots of things work: choose one that works for you.

Here are a few simple hints that apply to most windows:
• Clean the windowsills and frames before the glass. Vacuum to remove loose dirt before wiping with a damp cloth.
• Start at the top and work down to avoid dripping onto clean windows.
• Don't clean windows in direct sunlight. The cleaner will dry before you can wipe it off, creating streaks.
• Make your drying strokes go up and down on one side of the window and back and forth on the other. That way you can tell which side the streaks are on.

The cheapest way to clean a window is to use plain water and newspaper. However, this method can get messy. So you may well prefer to use paper towels or a soft, lint free cloth or pad for the final wipe down. Apply the water with a sponge or squeegee, available at hardware stores. Dip the squeegee into a bucket of water, picking up just enough water to wet the window without drenching it. Then wad up the newspaper a little and rub the window until it's dry.

Paper towels also work but are expensive and wasteful. A chamois cloth is as good.

SPOTLESS SASHES

Many sash windows are now made so they can be tilted inward for cleaning. But if you don't have that kind, you can still clean both sides from inside the house – provided both upper and lower windows move fully, as they're supposed to. Take care at all times: but no major leaning out is ever required. Here are instructions for reaching the outside of both windows.

1 Pull the top window all the way down. (It will be on the outside.)

2 Reach through the opening to clean the top part of the outside. Wash, then wipe.

3 Raise both windows all the way to the top.

4 Reach through the opening to clean the bottom part of the outside window.

5 Lower the inside window enough to reach the outside window and push it all the way to the bottom.

6 Now reach through the opening to clean the top part of the inside window.

7 Raise the outside window all the way to the top and lower the inside window as much as possible while leaving room for your arm to pass through the opening.

8 Reach through the opening to clean the bottom part of the inside window.

For added cleaning power on dirty glass, here are some formulas to try:
• For grease or hard-water deposits, use 100ml of white vinegar in 2 litres of water plus a squirt of washing-up liquid. For speed, pour this into a spray bottle.
• For grime, grease or smoke, use 100ml of clear ammonia in a litre of water.
• For tough jobs, you can add methylated spirits. But it will need rinsing off afterwards, so only do this if all else fails. Mix up 250ml of methylated spirits with 40ml of clear ammonia and a drop of washing-up liquid in 2 litres of water.
• For the ultimate dirty window, get a specialist window cleaning product from a car supply shop. This is pricy and will need rubbing in, then rinsing off. So it is just suitable for a small area.

Trouble shooting tip
• To remove hard-water mineral spots, use straight vinegar.
• For scratches in glass, rub a little toothpaste into the scratch and polish with a soft cloth.
• To peel off paint and stuck-on adhesives, scrape with a razor blade. Don't use a putty knife, however, because it's duller and can damage the glass.

Using a squeegee to clean windows is the method preferred by many people, including most professional window cleaners. Buy a good squeegee with a removable rubber blade so that it can be replaced as it wears. The main disadvantage of a squeegee is that it's impractical on small panes of glass – although you can

buy smaller, 10cm ones at hardware shops. When using a squeegee, technique is important.

1 First, wet the squeegee.

2 Draw it across the top of the pane.

3 Start the squeegee at the bottom edge of that swath and draw it down one side of the glass to about 4cm from the bottom. Repeat this step, overlapping each stroke as you work your way across the whole window.

4 Draw the squeegee across the bottom of the pane.

5 Wipe the squeegee on a cloth between each stroke.

6 Use a clean cloth to wipe the window edges, if necessary.

7 On very large windows, wash and dry the top half, before moving on to the bottom half.

Laundry

Everyone has clothes to clean. Not everyone cleans them as well as they could. They wing it or get by on the bare minimum. This chapter will help you to do a better, more thorough job on your laundry. You will be more knowledgeable, more confident and more efficient. More importantly, your clothes and household linens will be cleaner, brighter, fresher and last for longer.

Sorting your laundry

Most of us put dark clothes in one pile, and whites in another. But if you really want to keep your clothes looking their best, it is well worth sorting them by similar fabrics and dirt level.

Sorting by colour Separate whites from colours and light colours from dark colours. This is most important if you want to choose different detergents, for instance a 'colour' product such as Ariel Colour, which doesn't contain optical brighteners and so won't dull coloured clothes. Read care labels to be on the look-out for garments that need to be washed separately. This is because the dye colours may run. You won't just find this with red or black tops. Even tiny amounts of a beige dye can transfer to other fabrics, making lighter clothes look discoloured and dingy.

Sorting by dirtiness Separate heavily soiled or greasy items from lightly soiled ones. Lightly soiled clothes can pick up some of this dirt and grease, making whites look grey or yellow and colours look dull. If you have a load of particularly dirty clothes, you should also put fewer of them in the machine and use the maximum dose of detergent.

Sorting by fabrics Separate out clothes that are loosely knit or woven and items that have delicate trimmings or unfinished seams that could fray. Wash those on a shorter cycle that features more gentle agitation. Also separate lint producers – such as fleece sweat suits, chenille items, new towels and flannel pyjamas – from lint attractors, such as corduroys, synthetic blends and dark things. In the long run, it is quicker to do more loads of washing than spend time getting pale lint out of a pair of corduroy trousers.

Getting ready to wash

Just a little careful preparation before you put your clothes in the washing machine is essential to get the cleanest clothes. Don't just chuck everything in and shut the door. A few routine steps – like checking pockets and so removing crayons from your child's trousers – can prevent a laundry disaster.

Empty pockets Be especially alert for tissues, which can also be wedged up sleeves or stuck in pockets. Keep a small brush handy to brush dirt and lint out of cuffs.

Close zips and Velcro This prevents snags and keeps Velcro from getting matted with lint and thread and so losing its effectiveness.

Bag tights Put tights, stockings and items with long ties, such as bikini tops, into a net washing bag to keep them from snagging and tearing. You can buy these these from **www.lakelandlimited.co.uk**

Getting tough with stains

It's always best to try to remove stains when they are fresh. From page 115 there are detailed techniques for removing stains at this stage.

Modern detergents are actually very good at shifting most stains. But if the staining is particularly bad and you don't feel confident that your detergent will shift it, try the following first.

Soak protein stains including egg, milk, faeces, urine and blood for half an hour in cold water, then run under a cold tap, gently rubbing the fabric together with your hands to loosen the stain. Avoid warm or hot water, which can 'cook' proteins, setting the stain permanently.

Pretreat oil and grease stains with liquid laundry detergent or pre-treatment spray applied directly to the stain.

Soak tannin stains such as coffee, tea, soft drinks, fruit and jam for half an hour in a solution of 1 teaspoon of liquid detergent (a biological one containing enzymes) per 2 litres of warm water. Do not use soap or a soap-based product. Soap can make the tannin stain harder to remove.

After washing in the machine check to see whether the stain has gone. If it hasn't, do not dry and especially do not tumble dry. Try again to remove the stain and then repeat washing.

All about washing machines

Most of us pick up our laundering skills in bits and pieces. Chances are, you may have missed out on some of the following essential tips.

Evenly distribute clothes in the washer The spin cycle relies on a balanced load. The best mix is large items such as sheets with smaller hand towels and socks.

Don't overload the machine The wash cycle depends on clothes rubbing together to remove dirt. If the drum is too full, the clothes will not have enough space to rub together. Powdered detergent may not have room to dissolve, and you may end up with clumps of white powder on your clothes. There must also be enough free-flowing water to carry away the dirt.

Check the maximum load Most are between 5–6kg. Considering a woollen jumper can weigh 1kg and a duvet cover 1.5kg, a full load soon mounts up.

Pick the right setting Most clothes use the normal or regular setting. Do use the gentle or delicate setting – sometimes marked as quick wash for lingerie, loose knits, washable woollens and synthetic fabrics that can get damaged by over-spinning.

Choose the right water temperature On many machines, the hot cycle draws directly from your household hot water supply, then heats it to the required temperature. This is usually a choice of 60 or 80°C, although pricier machines have an override, that lets you choose exactly the temperature that you want for every wash programme. The warm 40°C wash on most machines takes water from the cold water supply, then heats it to the desired temperature. Check care labels to set the temperature.

• **Hot (95–60°C)** Only use the 95°C option for 'boil wash' safe items, such as white cotton sheets. The 60°C hot wash is hot enough for whites and colourfast fabrics and heavily soiled clothes that say on the care label that they can withstand this temperature. Water this hot can kill most bacteria (not true at 40°C). When starting a hot-water load, make sure no one is about to take a shower or bath otherwise they may get no hot water.

• Warm (40°C) Use for noncolourfast fabrics, moderate soiling, synthetics, crease-free fabrics, knits, silks and woollens. Most leading detergents are designed to be as effective at this temperature. So it can make sense to choose this most of the time: your clothes will look just as good and you'll save energy and money on fuel bills by not over-heating the water.

• Cold (30°C) Use for dark or bright colours that you know will bleed. Powdered detergent will not dissolve well at low temperatures; use liquid detergent instead.

Add the right amount of detergent Read the packet and use the measuring scoop. Or switch to tablets (powder) or liquid capsules. The main cause of clothes coming out yellow, grey and dingy is not using enough detergent.

Although detergents and powder both work well, liquid detergents are best with cool washes and on oily stains. Powders will remove ground-in dirt and mud. Biological is always best for cleaning, but if you have sensitive skin, use non-bio instead.

Soften the water In hard water areas your clothes may come out grey and dingy and feeling rough. Other symptoms are rings around the water line in the bath, white residue around taps and drains, and soaps and shampoos that don't lather well. The easiest solution is just to add a little more detergent. A water softening product, such as Calgon, added to each wash will stop mineral deposits building up.

Laundry extras

These days, there are many products you can use in the wash to enhance the look and feel of your laundered items. All-fabric bleaches, softeners and wash-boosters are among the most popular. Bleaches come in two varieties: traditional, powerful chlorine bleach and the newer, gentler all-fabric bleaches.

Chlorine bleach (sometimes labelled as sodium hypochlorite) is the most effective whitener and sanitiser but it is extremely strong and can fade colours and weaken fibres. It does have a place as a pre-soak for whites that are very soiled or greying. But use it with care. Never pour full-strength liquid chlorine bleach directly into the washing machine. Always dilute, then dispense it through a machine's bleach dispenser, following the instructions on the container. Don't soak cottons for more than 15 minutes. If the stain remains after 15 minutes, it can't be removed using this solvent. Don't use on silk, wool, Lycra, polyurethane foam, rubber or anything with rubber or Lycra.

All-fabric bleach sometimes called oxygen bleach, contains hydrogen peroxide, or another chlorine substitute. They are less harsh and are safe for some coloured fabrics. At the same time, they are not as powerful or fast-acting as chlorine bleach. Oxygen bleach is used in many commercial wash boosters. Ace Wash Booster goes directly into the wash cycle in a dispenser ball. It whitens whites and brightens colours, rather than fading them, as a cholorine bleach would.

Enzyme pre-soaks are good for loosening and removing stains, especially protein stains like milk, egg, urine and faeces. When added to the wash cycle, they act like boosters to improve the washing. Many are quite safe for delicate fabrics and contain no bleach.

Prewash stain removers are often spray products containing some combination of concentrated detergents, alcohol, mineral spirits or enzymes. They are good for removing oily or greasy stains from synthetic fibres. Their great advantage is that you can directly target the stain. A product like Shout Stain Removing Spray is effective even at low temperatures.

Detergent boosters increase stain and soil-removal action, altering the pH of water and brightening clothes. Glo-White Ultra Wash Booster works for colours as well as whites. With a good detergent and not too many clothes in the wash, boosters aren't generally needed.

Water softeners are quick fixes for hard water. Added directly to the wash or rinse cycle of your machine they soften the water, making the detergent work more effectively.

Fabric softeners in liquid form are added to the final rinse cycle or come in sheets for the drier. They make fabrics softer and fluffier, reduce static cling and creasing, and make ironing easier. The latest products – fabric conditioners sealed in one dose capsules – are handy if you tend to slosh in too much fabric conditioner.

Starches and fabric finishes are rarely used these days. Used either in the final rinse or after drying, they temporarily stiffen fabrics, so they look crisp and fresh.

Drying laundry

A tumble drier will dry laundry in a couple of hours. But before you start tumbling, spend a little time to do the following.

Check clothes for stains before drying. If you overlook a stain you may set it permanently by drying at a high temperature. Treat and rewash any stains.

Shake damp items to loosen them and helps them dry faster and more thoroughly. Pull out anything that needs to be line or flat dried and has a 'no tumble drying' symbol on it, such as woollens or bras.

Don't overload the drier A drier needs some airflow to do its work. A packed drier will take longer and crease clothes.

Don't underload the drier The tumbling effect is reduced in driers with small loads, prolonging the drying period. If you must dry only one item, add a few clean towels of a similar colour to the wet garment to improve the process.

Use the right setting Most driers have the following automatic settings.
• Regular for all-cotton fabrics.
• Permanent press for synthetics.
• Cool for lingerie, washable woollens and heat-sensitive items.
   The permanent press cycle typically features a cool-down period after the drying is completed to reduce creasing.

Avoid overdrying This causes shrinkage, static build-up, and creasing. Overdrying can actually set creases, making them harder to remove.

To reduce creasing remove items from the drier as soon as they are dry. Hang up or fold as soon as possible. Remove permanent press items while damp and hang on a rustproof hanger. Close buttons and snaps, straighten trouser creases, and brush out any wrinkles.

Clean the lint filter after each use. Not doing so is a serious fire hazard. A filter without lint also means a better airflow and improved drying performance.

Use a mesh bag for drying tights to protect them from snagging.

For items that call for flat drying such as sweaters, squeeze out excess water, but don't wring, or you may cause creasing. Roll the garment in a clean, dry towel to absorb water. Then shape and lay out flat on a dry towel or drying rack. Over the bath is ideal.

Outdoor drying

Even if you have a tumble drier, your clothes and bedding will appreciate the full, fresh dry off you can only get from the wind blowing them dry.

Turn clothes inside out if it's sunny it will stop coloured garments fading in strong sunlight.

Peg with care Avoid making ridges by pegging trousers at the waistband and shirts at the underarm seam, rather than on the shoulders.

Check your washing regularly to avoid over-drying. Synthetics and nylons will dry before cotton items.

Wipe down the washing line if you haven't used it in a while, to avoid a line of dirt across your freshly-washed clothes.

Easy ironing

Ironing can be a real chore, but you can cut down the time you spend at the ironing board with these tips.

Wash and dry your clothes correctly Don't overload your drier and don't over-dry your clothes. Sometimes it's enough to smooth a garment (such as a t-shirt, sweater, jeans) with your hands and fold it or hang it. Dry things well, and you will cut ironing time down considerably.

Try touch-up ironing Instead of ironing the whole garment, run the iron over the collar and cuffs?

Read care labels Look out for advice on any parts of the garment that should not be ironed – for instance, a specially-finished embroidered section.

Keep your ironing board and iron clean Wash the ironing board cover regularly; clean the iron soleplate (see page 40). Otherwise, you may stain clothes the next time you iron them.

Sort items by ironing temperature Start with low-temperature fabrics, such as silks and synthetics and move on to cottons and linens that need a hot iron. Iron clothes while damp since creases are not as set in the fabric. Hang garments immediately to help them stay fresh and pressed.

To keep creasing to a minimum, start with small areas, such as cuffs, collars and sleeves, and then work your way to the larger areas. Iron lengthwise on fabric to prevent the fabric from stretching.

Never iron stains Check very carefully for stains before ironing. The heat will set the stains permanently.

Know your fabric

There's no substitute for checking the care label, but items you already own may still not have their labels attached. Consider these tips for specific materials.

Acetate Most acetates are dry-clean only. For those that are washable, hand-wash in warm water with mild suds. Don't soak items with collars. Do not wring and lay flat to dry. While still damp, press inside out with a cool iron. For a 'finishing' iron, place a cloth between your garment and the iron. When removing stains never use acetone, or a nail polish remover containing acetone, as it will dissolve the fibres.

Acrylic Machine-wash, using a warm-water setting and fabric softener. Tumble dry at a low temperature. To avoid creasing, remove from the drier as soon as they are dry. When hand-washing, use warm water and a mild detergent. Rinse and gently squeeze out the water, smooth out the garment, and dry on a rustproof hanger. Lay sweaters and knits flat to dry. When ironing, use a moderately warm iron.

Alpaca Nearly all alpaca can be dry-cleaned, and some knitted items can be gently washed by hand in cool water with a mild, undyed soap or shampoo. Don't twist or wring and lay out flat to dry, pressing with a dry towel to remove excess water. Touch up with a cool iron.

Cashmere Knitted cashmere can be hand-washed. Use a natural, undyed soap and cool water. Move the sweater around in the cool water for a few minutes. Rinse repeatedly until the rinse water is clear. Lay out the sweater to dry, pressing it with a dry towel to remove excess water. If you need to touch it up with an iron, do so carefully, using a pressing cloth.

Cotton Unless the care label says otherwise, machine-wash pure cotton in high temperatures using a good detergent. With cotton-mixes, you'll need to follow the wash instructions for the less robust nylon or polyester. You can use chlorine bleach safely on cotton whites but only in short bursts: never soak for more than 15 minutes, since the bleach will break down the fibres. Use all-fabric bleach on dyed cottons. Cotton is absorbent and takes a while to dry. Press with a hot steam iron.

Linen You can wash some varieties of linen, but others should be dry-cleaned. Linen has a natural pectin that keeps it stiff and crisp. Washing removes the pectin, making it softer. So if you prefer crisp linen, have it dry-cleaned. Otherwise, machine-wash in warm water and tumble dry, and consider adding starch. Linen always creases; use a steam iron on medium or high heat.

Lycra Machine or hand-wash most items containing Lycra. Never use chlorine bleach. Either let drip dry or put in a drier on a low

setting. When ironing, use a low temperature setting and iron lightly using swift strokes.

Nylon Machine-wash in warm water. To reduce static cling, add a tumble drier conditioning sheet to the drier and remove clothes from the drier as soon as they have finished drying. If you need to iron nylon, use a warm iron – it can scorch easily and quickly at hotter temperatures.

Polyester Most polyester can be washed or dry-cleaned. Wash in warm water and tumble dry at a low temperature setting. To prevent pilling and snagging, turn knits inside out. To reduce static cling, use a drier sheet and remove garments as soon as they have dried.

Rayon (viscose) There are more and more washable rayons on the market. But dry-clean only rayon that gets wet can bleed dyes, shrink and grow stiff. Washable rayon is typically hand-wash only. Wash in lukewarm or cool suds, squeezing the suds through the fabric, and rinse. Never wring or twist. Shake out or smooth the garment and hang it on a rustproof hanger to dry. Lay sweaters flat. While the garment is still damp, iron inside out on a low heat. Use a pressing cloth to finish on the right side.

Silk Most silk is dry-clean only, since laundry detergents can harm silk. If the care label says that hand-washing is safe, use a mild soap and lukewarm water. Never use bleach with silk. When ironing, iron inside out on a low heat and use the iron lightly.

Wool If there is no care label guidance, dry-cleaning is safest: hot water on wool can lead to serious permanent shrinkage. However, most of the knitwear you can buy today is washable, some if it even by machine. If it's a hand-wash item, use warm water and a mild detergent that contains no bleach. Don't soak. Rinse thoroughly. To dry, roll in a clean towel and squeeze out excess water. If you think that the item may shrink, trace round it onto a piece of wrapping paper before washing. Put a piece of clear plastic over it (to stop dye transfer). Lay the washed item onto the template and pull it back to its original shape, but no more.

THE LOWDOWN ON LABELS

Sewn-in care labels are a legal requirement in all clothing sold in the UK and EC states. Most, but not all, countries have similar laws. In theory, even that ethnic shirt you pick up on holiday should have a care label. The labels give instructions for the best way to care for a garment, including how to properly clean, dry and iron and what techniques and products to avoid.

Here is a handy explanation of the symbols:

WASHING	DRYING

MACHINE WASH

 Normal
The number shows the maximum temperature for safe washing. Can cope with a full spin.

 Use a programme suitable for synthetics.
Reduced spin.

 Gentle/delicate/wool programme.

 Hand wash. Look for maximum temperature in the wash bowl.

Warning signs

 Do not wash.

BLEACH

 Any bleach (when needed)

 Chlorine bleach may be used

Warning signs

 Do not bleach

DRY CLEANING

 Normal cycle Dry-clean.

Warning signs

 Do not dry-clean.

TUMBLE DRY

 May be tumble dried.

 Tumble dry on high setting.

 Tumble dry on low setting.

Warning signs

 Do not tumble dry.

AIR DRY

 Line dry/hang to dry.

 Drip dry.

 Dry flat.

IRONING

 Hot iron – maximum setting.

Medium iron.

Cool iron – Use minimum setting.

Warning signs

Do not iron.

Problems and solutions

Ordinary dirt and difficult stains are one thing. But sometimes even when there is no definable stain, clothes just don't turn out right. Here are some common problems and the likely solutions to the problems.

Laundry comes out grey or yellow You may need to increase the amount of detergent in the next load, use a detergent booster or increase the temperature of the wash water. But the grey could be from dye that has bled from darks to lights, suggesting you need to sort better.

Detergent residue on clothes The powdered detergent isn't dissolving properly. Put fewer items into the washing machine. Use liquid detergent with 30°C cycles. If the problem is caused by hard water, remove hard-water residue from clothes by soaking them in a solution of 200ml white vinegar per 7.5 litres warm water. Rinse and rewash.

There's lint on your clothes You need to sort clothes better. Separate fleece-backed sweatshirts, chenille, new towels and flannel pyjamas, from corduroys, synthetics and dark fabrics. To remove the lint, use a lint roller or pat with the sticky side of masking or packing tape. Make sure pockets are empty of tissues and other paper before washing and make sure the washer and drier lint filters are free of lint.

Pilling This is most common with synthetic fabrics and makes even new items look old and shabby. Try turning synthetic clothing inside out before washing. You can also wash synthetics together in a gentler, shorter cycle. Using a liquid detergent will help. It is possible to remove pills but be aware that it is also very easy indeed to create holes in the fabric beneath. So going at your own risk, and with care, pull fabric tight over a curved surface and carefully shave the pills off with a safety razor or a battery-powered pill remover available from haberdashers.

Cleaning your equipment

Washing machines

Cleaning the exterior of your washer or drier The most common spots are blotches of detergent, fabric softener or bleach. Wipe them up with a cloth dipped in a solution of warm water and mild washing-up liquid, which will vanquish dirt and accumulated dust.

To clean inside your washing machine wipe down the inside of the door using the same solution of warm water and mild washing-up liquid on the cloth that you used on the exterior. Use an old toothbrush to clean the crevices of the moulded frame around the door. If you have a removable detergent cup, take it out to clean it. If it's built in, clean it as thoroughly as you can, using a pipe cleaner, if necessary.

To get rid of musty odours, run the machine through a wash cycle without any clothes in it. Use the hottest temperature setting and a medium or high water level. While the washing machine is filling, pour in 200ml of bleach. Do this once a year.

Tumble driers

When cleaning a drier, the most important task is to clean the filter. Driers work by heating air, drawing it across your wet clothes to sop up the moisture and pushing the soggy air outside through a vent or condensing it into water and storing this in a tank that you empty regularly.

The most modern tumble driers have alerts to remind you to clean the filters that collect lint before or after every load of clothes. Check the manual to find out how to remove the filter. Hold it over the bin, whilst scraping the lint off the filter with your hand. If some of the lint remains stuck, you might take the filter to a sink and clean it with warm water and a mild washing-up liquid.

To remove crayon marks from inside the drier, run it empty for five minutes to soften up the marks. Then wipe them away with a cloth dipped in a solution of water and washing-up liquid.

Irons

To remove stuck on fibres, heat the iron until the fibres liquefy. Then, on nonstick and aluminium or chrome soleplates, use a wooden spatula or ice lolly stick to scrape off the fibres. Run the iron over a towel or other rough material that the remaining fibres will be able to stick to. If you don't know what's stuck on your soleplate and the mark doesn't liquefy when you heat the iron, use any hot iron cleaner, available at fabric shops and hardware stores.

If the stain still remains on an aluminium or chrome soleplate, make a soft paste of bicarbonate of soda and water. Rub it on a cool iron with a soft cloth, then wipe it off with another damp cloth. Don't use this method on nonstick soleplates.

On Teflon or metallic-coated nonstick surfaces, a damp cloth should wipe off any water marks and a wooden spatula should remove any fibre stains. Should any marks still remain, rub a nylon scouring pad on the iron's soleplate when it's cool.

To clean sticky, oil-based residue from an aluminum or chrome soleplate, spray all-purpose cleaner onto a cold iron and rub with a soft cloth. Remove the cleaner by rubbing with a wet cloth. Before using the iron again, heat it and rub the soleplate on a rag to remove any residue.

To clean acetate or nylon use acetone on a cloth and rub the affected area of the cold soleplate until the melted residue is gone.

To clean a waxy stain heat the iron as hot as possible and iron a completely dry newspaper until the wax is gone.

To remove burned lint, use the iron's 'burst of steam' feature as directed.

To prevent stains forming on the soleplate use a pressing cloth, a lightweight pure cotton cloth, which will act as a barrier between the iron and your clothing.

To clean the iron's steam chamber, check the guidelines about whether to use distilled or tap water. Unplug and fill the iron with water. Then plug in the iron and, depending on your model, either turn the iron to its cleaning mode function or to the steaming feature. Hold the steaming iron over a sink, with the soleplate face down, until the steam stops. Unplug and leave it in the sink for another half hour to dry.
  Or place the iron face down on a heatproof cooking rack while it steams. The steam will remove lint, dirt, dust and mineral deposits. Wipe with a dry cloth.

If the steam-cleaning technique doesn't remove the mineral deposits, use vinegar if your manufacturer's instructions permit it. Pour white vinegar into the steam chamber and steam it through the vents. Rinse and refill the chamber with water. Let the water steam through the iron to remove all the vinegar. If you're not careful about removing the vinegar, it may stain your clothes the next time you use the iron and it can damage the interior of the iron.

If the steam vents on the soleplate become clogged, push a paperclip into the holes to reopen the vents before steaming the iron.

Always dry and cool your iron before putting it away and store it in an upright position on the heel rest.

Kitchens

These days, most of us consider the kitchen to be the hub of the home. We cook, eat and socialise there. But its multipurpose nature means that the potential for all kinds of dirt, grease and grime is quite frightening. In this chapter you'll find the best ways to clean your kitchen surfaces, large appliances such as ovens, fridges and freezers, as well as the many items we use to prepare, cook, serve and store food, and even how to clean your food so that you know that it is safe.

Kitchen cabinets

To routinely clean the cabinet exteriors, dust with a clean cloth regularly and wipe with a damp cloth periodically. Never use abrasive cleaners or scourers on kitchen cabinets. Also avoid using your dishcloth, because it may contain grease or detergents that can add streaks and smears.

To wipe away the stains around handles on doors and drawers – you'll need to use a heavy-duty cleaner, because those stains will probably be the most troublesome, being a mixture of skin oils, food smears and softened finish. On cabinets made of plastic laminate, metal or glass, try a strong all-purpose household cleaner. Spray it onto a cloth or sponge and apply to the dirty areas. Let the cleaner sit for a few minutes and then wipe it off with a rinsed-out cloth or sponge. Wipe again with a dry cloth.

To clean wood cabinets, first try a little washing-up liquid applied directly to a cloth or sponge. Rub into the dirty areas around the hardware. Then wash the entire cabinet with an oil soap solution. Use 60ml of oil soap (such as Pledge Soapy Cleaner for wood and laminate surfaces) to 4 litres of water. Apply with a cloth dipped in the solution and wrung out. Then go over the cabinets with a cloth dampened in plain water, followed by a dry cloth.

To protect the surface of the cabinets, apply a wax suitable for your cabinets' material. Car wax or other paste waxes work well on wood. Once a year, apply thinly to a clean surface with a clean cloth and then buff.

To clean cabinets with glass doors, wash the glass with a cloth or paper towel sprayed with a little glass cleaner. Don't spray cleaner, or even plain water, directly onto the glass – it can drip down and damage the surrounding wood.

To clean the shelves, use the same methods as for exterior surfaces. Shelves need thorough cleaning only once or twice a year if you clean up any spills as soon as they happen. To remove an old spill, sprinkle with bicarbonate of soda and wipe with a damp cloth.

Worktops

Keeping worktops pristine serves two purposes: your kitchen looks nicely kept and, since this is where most food preparation takes place, you are helping to cut levels of bacteria for bacteria and so reducing the risk of possible contamination and sickness.

Worktops have come a long way since Formica, a plastic laminate, reigned supreme. Today, the most common type is a solid-surface synthetic. (Corian is one popular brand.) Other popular types are marble, granite and engineered or synthetic stone – and wood. It's worth reading the manufacturer's directions for cleaning your kind of worktop.

General maintenance calls for removing the stuff on top first, then cleaning up surface dirt and crumbs with a soft-bristled brush or handheld vacuum. Wet a nylon-backed sponge with soapy water (washing-up liquid in warm water) and use the soft side of the sponge to wash the counter, backsplash included. Let the soapy water sit on the surface a few minutes to soften any spots. Switch to the scrubbing side to remove any intransigent spots. Rinse with warm water and buff dry with a clean, lint-free towel. Or squirt with a multi-purpose kitchen cleaner and wipe clean with a sponge. Most will not need rinsing.

Plastic laminates, such as Formica, should not be cleaned with abrasives. Mop up spills immediately with a sponge, then use a soapy sponge or all-purpose kitchen cleaner. For obstinate stains, try one of these approaches:
• Sprinkle with bicarbonate of soda and rub with a soft, damp cloth. Rinse and dry with paper towels or a cloth.
• Make a paste of lemon juice and cream of tartar, spread on the stain and let sit for 15 minutes. Rinse and dry.
Laminates need a gentle touch as they age. They are susceptible to chipping, scratching and losing their shine.

Solid-surface synthetics, such as Corian, can withstand light abrasion. Wet a scrubbing sponge or sprinkle a mildly abrasive cleaner, such as Cif (without bleach), on a damp sponge and apply with gentle pressure. Rinse with water on a sponge and dry with a soft cloth.

Stone worktops, usually those made of marble or granite are rather delicate. If you are buying a new kitchen and want quick, easy cleaning, don't go for these. But if you already have them in your house, here's what to watch out for. Acid etches marble and anything greasy stains granite.

When cleaning marble and granite, never use anything abrasive. Dust with a clean, dry rag. Wipe up spills immediately to avoid staining. First try using only warm water, and wiping with a soft cloth or sponge. Let caked-on food soak for a while before wiping. You should be able to remove spills, crumbs, sauces and other substances this way. If not, then add a little washing-up liquid to the water. Rinse well with plenty of clean water. Too much soap can leave a film or cause streaking. Avoid stronger cleaning products, such as bath and tile cleaners or scouring powders, which can stain or scratch.

To maintain stone worktops:
• Blot up spills at once with paper towels. Don't wipe – that will only make it worse. Flush the spot with warm water and mild soap, rinsing several times before drying with a soft cloth.
• Use coasters, trivets or place mats under glassware and dishes to protect surfaces from scratching. Heat damages marble, so never set anything hot on it.
• Stone countertops are sometimes sealed with a penetrating commercial sealant. Make sure that wherever you prepare food, the sealant is non-toxic. Vegetable oil is an effective non-toxic and homespun coating for food preparation areas.

Engineered stone usually resembles granite but requires no sealant and little extra care. Wash with soap and water and an all-purpose kitchen cleaner.

Wooden worktops Most will be treated with a tough laminate layer. But if you have untreated wood, go easy. To avoid scratching, do not use abrasive cleaners. Instead, use a soapy liquid cleaner that is especially for wood or dilute washing-up liquid. Always dry scrupulously afterwards. You will do the most damage if you leave wood wet. Regularly treat the wood with wax to prevent cracking.

Sinks

With all the soap and water that flow through your sink, you would think it would be clean all the time. But soapy deposits, food stains, rust and water spots have a way of accumulating quickly and creating a dirty scum.

For general cleaning of any sink, use a squirt of washing-up liquid and scrub the sink with a soft sponge. Rinse away residue. Don't use an abrasive cleaning agent or applicator, because it will scratch. A non-abrasive cleaner, like Astonish or Chemico will work on stubborn stains.

For a lightly stained porcelain sink, try one of these treatments:
• Rub a freshly cut lemon around the sink to cut through the grease. Rinse with running water.
• Sprinkle bicarbonate of soda around the sink and then rub it with a damp sponge. Rinse with vinegar or lemon juice to help neutralise the alkaline cleaner and then rinse with running water.
• Make a paste the consistency of toothpaste with bicarbonate of soda and water and gently rub the sink with a sponge or soft nylon brush. Polish with a paper towel or soft cloth.

Never use scouring powders or steel wool, because they will scratch.

Clean stainless steel sinks with a solution of warm water and a squirt of washing-up liquid, using a soft cloth or sponge. Always scrub in the direction of the stainless steel grain. Rinse with a cloth or sponge and clear water. Polish dry to avoid spotting, using paper towels or a cloth. For more cleaning power, use a solution of 1 part white vinegar and 3 parts water or scrub with a paste made of bicarbonate of soda and hot water.

To remove rust from stainless steel sinks, wipe WD-40 on the rust mark with a cloth and rinse thoroughly.

To remove water spots from any sink, use a cloth dampened with vinegar.

For a sparkling white ceramic sink, place paper towels across the bottom and saturate them with household bleach. Let it sit for 30 minutes and rinse with running water. Note: do not use bleach in coloured

porcelain sinks, because it will fade the colour. Clean these sinks with mild liquid detergents, vinegar or bicarbonate of soda.

For a sparkling metal sink, use a specialist chrome and metal cleaner. Apply then polish dry using a tea towel.

Stains in Corian-type sinks can be removed with toothpaste or a paste of bicarbonate of soda and water. Gently scrub the paste on with a white scrubbing pad. Your last resort is scrubbing very gently with very fine wet-or-dry glasspaper. Scrubbing too hard could wear a groove in the Corian. Polish the cleaned spot with a special polish made for Corian surfaces.

Water spots that have etched themselves into a sink's porcelain are extremely difficult to remove. Buff such spots out with a polishing compound as soon as you notice the spots. Use rouge with porcelain sinks.

To cover a chip or scratch on a white porcelain surface – including sinks, tubs and appliances – buy a container of white enamel paint at a DIY store. Following the package directions, paint over the mark with a small artist's brush, let it dry, rub with fine glasspaper and paint again. Repeat the process until the painted area is even with the surrounding surface. Or buy a porcelain repair kit, which will include filler, hardener, cleaner and glasspaper.

Dish drainers

Wash a dish drainer periodically in warm water with washing-up liquid, using a clean sponge. Do it separately, not while you're washing other dishes, since harmful bacteria can taint the dishes you are trying to clean. Use a scrubbing brush to remove stuck-on food and mould. Air-dry upside down on a clean towel. Disinfect the dish drainer every few weeks by soaking it in a solution of 40ml of bleach to every 5 litres of water.

Drains

If you have a slow-moving drain, it means sludge is building up in the pipe. When that happens, pour 100g salt into the drain, followed by 100g bicarbonate of soda. Then pour a full kettle of boiling water down the drain.

The abrasive salt and bicarbonate of soda will break down the blockage. If the problem is congealed grease, the clogging will loosen immediately. Don't turn on the tap for several hours, if possible. The longer you can go without diluting the mixture, the more effectively it will work.

If matted hair wedged down the pipework is the problem, you'll need a stronger solution. This one will work: dissolve 30g of Dri Pak Soda Crystals in a litre of water and pour it slowly down the drain. Let it work for 10 minutes; then run hot water until the drain seems clear.

If it is the waste-disposal unit drain that is slow, it is probably blocked with larger food particles. To cure the problem, first pull out the drain trap (the little basket-like object that sits in the drain hole at the bottom of the sink). Hold it inside the kitchen rubbish bin and tap it to loosen the debris trapped inside it. Replace the drain trap, twisting the knob to the closed position and fill the sink with warm water to a depth of 10cm. Add 100g of bicarbonate of soda. Turn on the waste disposal unit and let it run for a couple of seconds before you twist the drain trap knob to the open position. The water pressure will push any remaining food particles through the drain trap and give the waste-disposer a good clean at the same time. Turn on the tap for running water and let the disposer run until you get a free-spinning 'all clear' sound.

GET RID OF DRAIN SMELLS

If you won't be at home for several days, make sure no food wastes that might start to smell are left in the disposer. To flush any residue, plug the sink, fill it with around 6cm of water and run the disposer while the water drains.

Waste disposal units

These small, but extremely useful kitchen appliances have their own built-in scrubbing action. To keep your unit smelling fresh and running properly, all you need are a few common household items.

To keep food waste from building up inside the unit, keep these rules in mind:
• Grind only small amounts of food at a time.
• After you've finished grinding food, run a steady, rapid flow of cold water for up to 30 seconds. Cold water solidifies fatty and greasy wastes so they will be chopped up and flushed down the drain.
• Don't pour oil or grease through the disposer.
• Don't grind large bones. (Small bones are safe and even help break up grease deposits.)
• Don't grind bulky, fibrous materials like sweetcorn kernels.
• Never put caustic soda or chemical drain cleaners into your disposal unit.

To remove fatty wastes that have built up inside the disposer, periodically grind a handful of ice cubes mixed with 100ml of bicarbonate of soda. Together the powder and cubes (which of course are cold) will safely scour the inside of the unit. To eliminate odours, grind lemon or orange peel through every so often.

Dishwashers

After each use, take the time to empty grunge from cutlery baskets, filters and check the spray arm. If you don't do this you will be washing the next load of dishes in the food residue from yesterday's load.

• When rinsing out the cutlery bucket, use the power of water and turn it upside down under a fast tap. This way, you'll propel dirt and food bits back out the way they came. Use a tooth pick to get out tiny particles of food that get trapped in the spray arm.

• Every month, run the dishwasher on empty – but with a full supply of dishwasher powder or tablets.

• To keep the dishwasher smelling fresh if you are not going to use it for a while, add in 100ml of white vinegar.

Fridges & freezers

Keeping your refrigerator and freezer clean is crucial to the hygiene of your food and your family's health. There are three major aspects to keeping refrigerators and freezers clean: removing dirt, killing germs and deodorising the interior.

Cleaning the fridge is only a half-hour job, so don't worry about keeping food cold. Empty one shelf at a time, so food on the other shelves can stay chilled.
   Remove the first shelf and spray it over liberally with a disinfecting all-purpose cleaner – Dettol make one – to vanquish the inevitable sticky spills. Alternatively, a squirt of white vinegar in a spray bottle will cut though grease. Use paper towels to wipe the shelf dry, then reinsert it in the refrigerator. Repeat the procedure with each of the other shelves.

A SWEET-SMELLING FRIDGE

To deodorise your refrigerator or freezer, open a box of baking soda, leave it inside, and change it every few months. This tried-and-trusted method will absorb most of the odours you don't want emanating from your fridge, but it may not go far enough to suit you. Leaving an egg cup of dried coffee also absorbs odours and brings the faint aroma of your favourite drink to the fridge that you may prefer.

To clean the drawers, pull them out of the fridge one at a time, place them in the sink and fill them with warm water and a squirt of washing-up liquid. Let the water sit for 10 minutes. Then pour this out, rinse with fresh water and wipe dry with a towel.

Meat and poultry juices dripping on refrigerator surfaces are potentially harmful vehicles for the spread of salmonella and *E. coli*. Even though a refrigerator's temperature is low, it doesn't stop the growth of all bacteria. And it doesn't kill bacteria that is already present.

So as you remove each shelf, spray the inside of the refrigerator with a disinfecting all-purpose cleaner. Just because it looks clean doesn't mean that it is clean.

Cleaning the freezer is simple if you have a self-defrosting model. Just put the food in the sink. Piling frozen items on top of each other will keep them cold.

Soak a sponge in warm water and squeeze out enough water so as not to create trickles that will add to your work. Wipe each rack in the freezer, top and bottom. If you have a thick, frozen spill, scrape it first with a stiff plastic spatula that has a thin edge (don't use metal) and then spot clean it with a soapy sponge.

To defrost the freezer, use your eyes to tell you when you need to do it (every three months, would be typical) and do it before there's a tremendous ice build up. If you don't, you're effectively reducing the size of your freezer.

• Switch the freezer off at the plug.
• Use a cool box to store frozen food. Pack it tightly, with items that thaw fastest, such as ice cream, in the centre.
• Leave the door open and put a thick towel tight up against the freezer in front of the door.
• Stand a tray under the drip edge at the base of the freezer (this is a pull out slot that will catch the thawing ice).
• Do nothing while the ice melts.
• Using more towels, mop up the water. When this is complete, turn on the freezer, put back the food and avoid opening the doors at all for as many hours as you can. This will help to bring the temperature down faster.
• If you really must speed up the process, stand saucepans of hot water inside the shelves of the freezer: this will make the ice melt faster.

Regularly cleaning the seals and door handles is perhaps the most important aspect of fridge cleaning. When you're preparing food it's best to wash your hands each and every time you handle raw meat. That's easy to forget in the midst of cooking however and when you transfer that contamination to the door handles, another family member who uses the refrigerator could pick up the germs. The solution is to keep a box or tube of all-purpose wipes (Dettol do some) near the refrigerator and make it a habit to wipe off the handle frequently.

Ovens

Proper cleaning improves your oven's efficiency, extends its life and, most importantly, reduces the risk of fire. Even if you have a self-cleaning or continuous-cleaning oven, neither of which is self-sufficient, some of the tips that follow will help you to clean it even better.

Wipe the exterior surfaces of your oven to remove food spills every time you wipe down worktops. All you need is a moist sponge. Make it a habit and you'll save time in the end, because even the exterior surfaces get warm enough to bake food on very quickly.

To clean the interior, start by removing all oven racks and grill pans. Wash them by hand in the sink. Use a solution of warm water and washing-up liquid. Scrub with a nylon-bristled brush or other gentle, non-metal scrubber. Anything abrasive, such as steel wool, will scratch the metal's finish, which can lead to rusting and will make food stick even more the next time.

To loosen baked-on deposits in a conventional (non self-cleaning) oven, fill a glass bowl with 100ml of full-strength ammonia. After making sure the oven is completely cool, put the bowl of ammonia in the oven, close the door and let it stand overnight. The fumes will release the bond between the crusty food and the oven interior. The next day, open the door and let the fumes dissipate. Then remove the bowl and wipe away the loosened food with a cloth or sponge.

To remove stubborn food that remains after the ammonia treatment, try scouring with a nonabrasive scrubber dipped in a solution of warm water and washing-up liquid. As with the racks and grill pans, avoid scratching the oven's finish. On flat surfaces, such as the door glass, try scraping with a plastic ice scraper – the kind you use on your car windshield.

A commercial oven cleaner is a last-ditch solution when cleaning a conventional oven. Follow the directions carefully and wear protective rubber gloves when applying. These products are strong and can be extremely harmful to humans. Never spray a commercial oven cleaner on a hot

oven, electric elements or oven lights. The heat will make the oven cleaner even more caustic than it is cold.

Help your self-cleaning oven by doing a little preparatory work. Self-cleaning simply means that it will break down food spills with temperatures as high as 480°C. But the high heat doesn't reach all parts of the oven and in areas such as the frame around the oven opening and the edge of the door outside the gasket, the self-cleaning cycle can actually bake food on even more. So clean those parts first with a nonabrasive scrubber dipped in a sudsy solution of hot water and washing-up liquid. Rinse well using a sponge and a bucket of clean water. Once the self-cleaning cycle is complete and the oven has completely cooled down, wipe out the ashy residue with a damp sponge.

Give your continuous-cleaning oven a human touch. The interior of this type of oven is coated with a chemical mixture that lowers the temperature at which heat will dissolve foods. So whenever you bake or roast at a temperature above 180°C (350°F, gas mark 4), you are breaking down food that has splattered on the walls or bottom. But major spills, especially those involving sugar, can cancel out the effect. So clean up all big spills at once.

Wipe out the entire oven occasionally using a nonabrasive scrubbing pad and warm water. Then run the oven empty for an hour or two at 240°C (465°F, gas mark 9) to break down any grease or food that the oven's normal cooking and cleaning cycle has not dealt with. Never use abrasive cleaners or cleaning tools in a continuous-cleaning oven.

Cleaning Aga and range cookers is even simpler – because the cooker is always on, you can only totally clean them whilst they are turned off for their annual service. What you can do in the meantime is to be scrupulous about keeping the enamel front and top clean. Use a non-abrasive cleaner, such as Astonish, that is safe for enamel. Take even more care of the steel tops: a microfibre cloth, just dampened, is best. For the cooking plates, use a stiff wire brush to scoop off burnt food.

Every year, when the oven is serviced and is completely cold, clean out the inside using a cloth dipped in a sudsy washing-up liquid solution.

Microwave ovens

Microwave ovens have revolutionised everyday cooking and fast preparation isn't their only virtue. Compared to conventional ovens, microwaves are very easy to clean.

To clean splashes of fresh food before they have had time to dry, simply wipe down the microwave's interior with a sponge or paper towel dipped in a mixture of washing-up liquid and water. Follow with a clean water rinse. Use the same method for washing removable trays or turntables in the sink.

To remove dried-on food, heat a bowl of water inside the microwave before cleaning. Heat 400ml of water for three to five minutes on high power. The steam will soften the dried food. Then wipe down the interior with a sponge or soft cloth.

To get rid of odours in the microwave, wipe the interior with a solution of 200ml warm water and 1 tablespoon of bicarbonate of soda. Rinse with warm water. Or combine 200ml

water with 100ml lemon juice in a bowl and heat it on high for three to five minutes. Let it stand in the microwave for five to ten minutes before removing.

To remove stains from the microwave's ceramic floor or turntable, make a paste of bicarbonate of soda and water and apply it to the stain. Let it sit until the stain disappears, then wipe it off and rinse with a wet sponge or cloth.

Clean the microwave door with paper towels and glass cleaner.

Small kitchen appliances

To clean a small electrical appliance first unplug it – and let it cool. Wipe down with a damp cloth. To remove dried on food, mix a solution of warm water and washing-up liquid. Keep the liquid away from the electronics of the appliance. Never put an appliance in water unless the instructions say it's safe to do so. Some appliances have washable parts that should be removed from the electronic base to make cleaning easier and safer. Below are the specifics of how to clean individual items

Can openers

Cleaning a handheld can opener is simple. Just wash it with the dishes, either by hand or in a dishwasher.

Cleaning an electric can opener is also easy, because most have blades or cutting assemblies designed to be removed and washed with the dishes. Older models may not have detachable blades. In that case, clean the cutting parts, being careful not to cut yourself, with a cloth dampened with water and a little washing-up liquid.

If you're dealing with accumulated dirt, scrub with an old toothbrush. Regular cleaning thereafter will keep the machine clean. To clean the machine's body, wipe it with a clean damp cloth with the unit unplugged. Never immerse an electric can opener in water.

Coffee grinders

Clean a coffee grinder after every use. Unplug the unit. Brush out the grinder with a pastry brush, old toothbrush or special coffee grounds brush, sold at kitchen stores and coffee shops. This doesn't have to be a big job – just make sure you leave the stainless steel inside the grinder shiny, so that tomorrow's batch of beans won't be sullied by stale grounds from yesterday's pot. Wash the plastic lid with a sponge in washing-up liquid and warm water; rinse and dry with a soft cloth.

Two more methods to try:
• Dampen a paper towel and swab the inside of the grinder.
• Run a small handful of uncooked white rice through the coffee grinder, especially if you use it for grinding anything other than coffee beans and need to totally remove traces of say, nuts, before you enjoy your next drink. Most coffee experts advise against using your machine for grinding dry spices, by the way, since the smells from grinding ingredients such as cinnamon sticks and dried basil are nearly impossible to get out.

Coffee makers

Clean your coffee maker at least once a month – if you use it every day – to rid it of hard water deposits, or every two months if you brew a pot less often.

Always check your owner's manual before embarking on any of the following cleaning methods. In general, no electric coffee maker should be immersed in water.

To clean an electric drip coffee maker
• Fill the water reservoir, half with cold water and half with white vinegar. Place a clean paper filter in the basket. Run the coffee maker through its entire cycle. Repeat the brewing cycle two more times, using plain water each time to flush out the remaining grains.
• Fill the reservoir with hot water and add a denture tablet. Run the machine through its complete brewing cycle, and then run it once more using plain water.
• Wash the coffee carafe in hot water with washing-up liquid and rinse with water. Then remove any other removable parts and do the same. You can wash these pieces in the top rack of the dishwasher, but their colours may fade. If you do, buff them with a soft, dry cloth.

Cleaning a home espresso machine Get into the habit of turning off the machine, removing the froth head, then rinsing it under warm water every time you use your machine. Wipe the steam wand with a damp cloth. Turn the power back on and set the selector control to the steam position briefly. The shot of heat will clear any milk remaining in the steam wand. Every so often, run water through the unit with the filter in place, but with no coffee. If the filter holes do get blocked, use a nylon washing-up brush to dislodge tiny, stuck pieces of coffee.

Food graters

To clean a grater, soak it in warm to hot, soapy water. Use a pan brush with short bristles or even an unused toothbrush for the smaller graters. To protect the bristles of your brush, hold the grater upside down and brush with a bottom-to-top stroke (the

opposite of the grating motion). You can put a grater in a dishwasher, as long as the grater isn't made of tin, which can quickly oxidise when it's not dried thoroughly.

To dry your grater, place it on a dish rack or a lint-free tea towel. If you're paranoid about a tin grater not drying sufficiently and possibly rusting, let it dry for 15 minutes in the oven on a low heat.

Food grinders

Because a food grinder is often used to process meat, poultry and seafood, proper cleaning is critical to prevent transmission of harmful bacteria, such as salmonella. The best grinders disassemble completely, allowing you to clean each piece thoroughly.

To clean the grinding plates, first soak in a solution of hot water and washing-up liquid to dislodge most of the food. You can finish the job in a dishwasher (always consult the manufacturer's instructions first), set on a hot cycle.

If you are cleaning the parts by hand, soak in 1 tablespoon of salt to 2 litres of cold water for 10 minutes to dislodge the food. Then scrub the plates and blade with a brush in hot, soapy water to kill bacteria. To help get meat or other remnants out of the holes in the plates, poke wooden kebab skewers through the holes.

Lay the parts on a cloth towel and let them air-dry fully. Or you can place the parts in an oven at a temperature of 65°C for 10 to 15 minutes. If you put aluminium alloy blades in the dishwasher, they willl

quickly start to rust when they sit and dry. Once the blades are dry, rub vegetable or salad oil lightly over them to protect them from rusting.

To clean a food grinder's motor unit, never immerse it fully in water. Instead, use a spray bottle to lightly mist on an anti-bacterial kitchen cleaner. Or make your own: use 10ml of bleach in 1 litre of warm water. Wipe off with a cloth.

Food processors

For general cleaning, rinse under a running tap on at full blast to remove stuck on food from the discs and blades.

If your recipe doesn't require the use of the feed tube on top of your food processor, cover the bowl with a strong piece of plastic wrap before locking on the lid. This will prevent splattering on the lid and minimise cleaning.

To clean the power unit of your food processor, turn it off and unplug the unit. Wipe it with a damp cloth. Wipe off the safety motor drive cover and reinstall it on the unit, if necessary. Never use coarse or caustic cleaning products on the power unit or immerse it in water.

To clean the attachments, put them in the dishwasher – all except the blades. Since items can shift in the dishwasher, the blades could bend, be dulled or be burned if they touch a heating element. Wash the blades in hot, soapy water, dry with a cloth and store for future use. Some experts also suggest hand-washing the plastic bowl of a food processor in hot, soapy water. This protects the bowl from the harsher dishwasher detergent, which can make the plastic brittle and prone to breakage. On some models, the plastic bowl has a safety spring located where the bowl attaches to the food processor. It's difficult to get this spring thoroughly dry, so after you've given the bowl a quick wipe, let it air-dry before reassembling the processor. Otherwise, the spring may rust.

Pressure cookers

When the pressure cooker forces hot air out, food particles can get trapped in the pressure gauge (the device that rattles when the cooker is doing its job). Clean the gauge after every use to keep stray food particles from turning into bacterial debris.

To clean out the pressure gauge, the best tool is a large safety pin. Work at the little hole from both sides. You'll be amazed at the dirt that you can force out.

Pay regular attention to the gasket, the rubber ring that seals the space between the cooker and the lid. If you don't keep it clean, food build-up can result in bacterial build-up. Remove the gasket, pour a little washing-up liquid into your hands, hold them under the tap until you have suds and then massage the gasket until you are confident that you have removed any residue. Be careful not to stretch the gasket unnecessarily while you wash it.

With repeated washing, the gasket can stretch and lose its shape. And a gasket that doesn't fit properly is useless. It can also get crunchy with wear, so after washing and drying, rub it with olive or vegetable oil. Don't use corn oil which can get sticky and actually attract debris. It's a good idea to keep an extra gasket on hand.

To clean the inside of the cooker, nothing works better than washing-up liquid, hot water, a plastic scrubbing sponge and a little muscle power.

Toasters

Turn bread into toast and you are bound to get crumbs. When the crumbs fall into the toaster, you need to get them out.

Empty the crumbs out of your toaster once every week or so. Some toasters have slide-out crumb trays; others have hinged doors that allow you to empty the crumbs. No matter what kind of toaster you have or what sort of mechanism it has for crumb

removal, always unplug the toaster before you start cleaning it.

If you can't get all the crumbs out, try disintegrating them with heat. Run the toaster empty on the hottest setting two or three times. This is also the principle behind self-cleaning ovens.

For hard-to-remove crumbs, use a clean, dry toothbrush. Again, be sure the toaster is unplugged. Loosen crumbs with the brush and then dump them out. Turn the toaster upside down and shake. Do it gently, being careful not to damage the heating element.

Wipe down the outside of the toaster with a damp cloth. Wipe around the control knobs. Add a dash of vinegar or squirt of washing-up liquid to the cleaning water for more cleaning power. For stainless steel toasters, polish with a stainless steel polish.

Cutlery

Rinse knives, forks and spoons under running water immediately after eating. You may not want to actually wash-up if, say, you're entertaining, but rinsing will remove food that might cause pitting or staining.

Be especially diligent about eggs, fruit juices, tomatoey foods, lemon, vinegar, salty foods (including butter), mustard, and salad dressings. Silver is most vulnerable, but stainless steel, despite its name, isn't completely immune to the threat of

corrosion. It's fine to soak both totally stainless steel and silver in warm water in a sink but don't soak hollow-handled utensils for long, lest it loosens the soldering.

Wash in the dishwasher along with your dishes, taking care not to spill detergent directly on the pieces, because it could pit or spot them. To get a beautiful finish however, you will have to carefully dry everything afterwards by hand using a soft dishcloth.

To brighten dull stainless steel cutlery: soak it in 4 litres of hot water mixed with 1 teaspoon of ammonia. Rinse with clear hot water and dry well with a clean cloth. Wash plate and sterling silver cutlery by hand. Use washing-up liquid in hot water. Rinse with clear hot water and dry immediately with a soft dishcloth. Don't use abrasive cleaners or scrubbers, such as steel wool. They will dull the finish.
The sulphur in eggs and egg products (such as mayonnaise) will cause silver to tarnish – instantly. So do pollutants in the air, but they work more slowly. Tarnish is not removed by regular washing and you will have to use a silver polish to remove it.

Clean pewter cutlery with a drop of methylated spirits on a soft cloth. Then follow up with the hot, soapy water treatment.

Cook's knives

For a bright and shiny knife at all times choose stainless steel. The problem with stainless is that when it loses its edge, it is not easy to sharpen. Or do you prefer a really sharp knife, one that you can easily sharpen? Choose carbon steel. The downside is that it's difficult to keep bright and shiny.

Wash knives immediately after use in a little washing-up liquid and hot water with a cloth or sponge. Rinse with hot water and wipe with a dry cloth.

To remove stains from a carbon steel blade, try a paste made of salt and vinegar. Rub it on the blade with a cloth. Or dip a slice of lemon into salt and rub that on the blade. Some stains will respond to a nylon scrubber or steel wool.

To shine the blade, use silver polish.

To protect the edges of knives, store them in a rack, a knife block or, if in a drawer, cover the blades with cardboard sleeves. You can make a sleeve by cutting a piece of cardboard (from a cereal box, for example) the length of the blade and twice as wide. Fold the cardboard in half lengthwise. Use tape to seal the side and one end. Insert the knife in the open end.

Dishes

Washing dirty dishes is a bit of a Herculean task; no matter how well you do it you always have to do it again after every meal. Here's the right way to wash up.

For everyday washing-up, fill the sink with moderately hot water and a squirt of washing-up liquid. If the dishes are particularly greasy, then add 2 tablespoons of white vinegar to the water.
Slide the dishes in edgewise into the water, to allow the temperature of the dish to equalise gradually. If very hot water hits a fragile dish too quickly, it may crack.
Once the dishes are stacked carefully in the sink, pour a little extra washing-up liquid on a sponge or dishcloth. Then resist the urge to scrub. Instead, wash in small circular motions. It might take longer than a vigorous scrubbing, but it will protect your china. Empty the water and fill again with plain water for rinsing.

When using the dishwasher:
• Load dishes so that they are separated and face the centre. Put glasses and cups between prongs, not over them.
• Don't position large dishes (or pots or pans) so that they block the spray arm, the spray tower, or the flow of water to the detergent dispenser.

• Use only dishwasher detergent in your machine. Follow the label directions for the amount. Less is needed if your water is soft (or artificially softened), more if it's hard.
• Use a rinse agent if your water is hard, but not if you have soft water.
• Don't pre-rinse moderately soiled dishes under the tap. Just scrape off any food.
• Use the hold-and-rinse cycle when you haven't got enough dishes to use the machine right away – or the noise of the dishwasher means you prefer to do it overnight or when you're out. A quick rinse stops odours building up.

China

Most china manufactured today is made to be functional as well as elegant and most china made in the past 25 years is dishwasher safe and says so explicitly on the bottom of the piece.

An exception is fine china with a band made of a precious metal such as platinum or gold where the high heat of the dishwasher's drying cycle may cause the metal to soften and small pieces become dislodged. Hand washing is also necessary for antique or hand-painted china. The force and heat of the dishwasher is too much for fragile pieces.

Washing china in the dishwasher does require a little extra care. Load carefully so plates and cups don't bump into each other and chip. Make sure aluminium utensils and foil containers don't rub against dishes during the wash cycle and make black or grey marks.

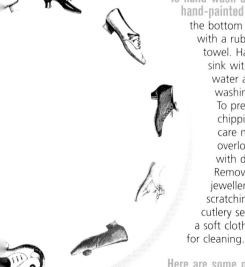

To hand-wash antique or hand-painted china, line the bottom of the sink with a rubber mat or towel. Half-fill the sink with warm water and a mild washing-up liquid. To prevent chipping, take care not to overload the sink with dishes. Remove rings and jewellery to prevent scratching and wash cutlery separately. Use a soft cloth or sponge for cleaning.

Here are some more tips:
• Wash or soak the items as soon after dining as possible, to

prevent the problem of dried-on food and staining. Acidic foods such as mayonnaise and eggs can damage the glaze if left on for long periods.
• To remove dried food, soak the china in a bowl of sudsy water and then scrub gently with a nylon scouring pad. Never use a metal pad, and avoid steel wool and gritty cleansers as well.
• Be careful when placing the dishes to dry to prevent scratches and chips. Prop carefully in a drying rack if possible.

Porcelain

Fine, dainty and often almost translucent, porcelain is one of the most fragile of all ceramics. How you clean depends on which finish your porcelain has – a bisque, or unglazed, finish or a glossy glazed finish.

To wash porcelain, use a washing-up bowl or a sink lined with a towel or rubber mat to protect against breakage.

To remove dirt and grime from either type of porcelain, first try a mild solution of warm water and washing-up liquid. Wipe with a cloth or scrub gently with a soft, nylon-bristled brush. A toothbrush is useful for nooks and crannies. Rinse well using clean water.

If that doesn't remove all the stains, try something stronger, such as an all-purpose household cleaner. Always rinse immediately and completely. These cleaning compounds can stain or etch porcelain. Air-dry in a dish rack or on a folded towel on the worktop.

To remove coffee or tea stains from the inside of porcelain cups or a porcelain teapot, scrub gently with a cloth or soft-bristled brush and a paste made from bicarbonate of soda and water.

Pottery

To clean glazed pottery – household items such as plates, mugs, serving trays and flower vases – proceed much as you would with your dishes. These items have been fired at up to more than 600°C, meaning they can stand up to any heat they will encounter in the dishwasher. Hand wash fragile or expensive pieces in the sink with warm water and washing-up liquid, so they don't get chipped in the dishwasher. A scrubber sponge will be fine for most hand washing, but the glaze will even stand up to the abrasion of a steel-wool pad.

To remove heavy dirt and grease, first dampen a cloth in methylated spirits, wipe it over the glazed pottery and then wash as usual in the dishwasher or sink.

Food

Before preparing food, wash your hands thoroughly with soap and water. Once they are completely clean, you are ready to prepare food.

• **To dry vegetables and fruits,** use a clean tea towel or paper towel or a lettuce spinner for greens. If preparing vegetables to cook, you don't need to dry them.
• **Cut away bruised or damaged areas** from fruits and vegetables with a sharp knife. Refrigerate fresh-cut items at once.
• **Rinse fish quickly in cold water** to remove ice, slime and loose small scales.

And here are some don'ts:
• **Don't use a brush** on soft-skinned vegetables or fruits. You'll damage them.
• **Don't use detergents or soap.** The produce could absorb the residues, which you could ingest.

To clean fruit and vegetables wash with plain water. Always wash all your fruit and vegetables – even organic ones. You are washing off chemical residue and germs that may have got onto your produce as it has been handled and stored. Though organic items may not have residual chemicals, they may have the same amount of dirt, dust and mould spores.

Cleaning specifics for certain foods:
• **For vegetables and fruits with a firm surface,** such as potatoes, celery and apples, use a vegetable brush to scrub the skin under running water.
• **For leaf vegetables and fruits with a soft skin,** such as peaches, strawberries and raspberries, rinse under running water.
• **Rinse mushrooms** very quickly under running water.

• **Don't wash raw poultry, beef, pork, lamb or veal** before using. You may think you're helping to make the meat safe, but you're not, you could be spreading germs. Cooking the meat at hot temperatures will destroy bacteria.
• **Keep raw meat, fish and poultry** in containers. Never place them directly on counters or the refrigerator shelves. Never let the juices of raw meat drip onto other foods and never use the same utensils on cooked foods that you have used for handling raw meat.
• **Don't wash eggs before storing or using them.** They will have been washed during commercial egg processing. Washing just removes more of the 'bloom', the natural coating on just-laid eggs that helps to prevent bacteria from permeating the shell.

Glassware

To clean a glass, just use hot water and washing-up liquid. But to get rid of streaks, spots and unappetising stains on the rim – and make your glassware really sparkle – you have to know how to dry them properly.

Clean glassware first when you are washing dishes by hand, since glasses are usually less dirty than pots, pans, plates and utensils. (If you don't clean the glasses first, then change the dishwater before you get to them. Otherwise, the glasses will end up dirtier than they were when you started.)

Use washing-up liquid mixed with hot water. Wash with a soft, clean sponge or dish cloth. Don't use an abrasive pot scrubber as it may scratch glass. Rinse with even hotter water – as hot as you can safely stand. Hot water not only helps cut grease, but it also beads up and steams off (the first step toward good drying is to dry fast). Avoid excessive suds, which make glasses harder to rinse and slippery to handle, which will increase the chances of their breaking or chipping.

No matter how well you've cleaned glassware, if there is slow-drying water left on your glasses, chances are it will leave streaks or spots. Fogging causes some of the worst spotting. To avoid the 'greenhouse effect' – when glasses placed upside down on their rims fog up inside – dry glasses upside down on a drying rack. If you don't have a rack, put them upright on a towel and make sure air can circulate inside the glass for rapid drying.

To remove the lime build-up that occurs when glassware is washed in the dishwasher, use a commercial rinse agent (such as Finish Lemon Rinse Agent) during the washing cycles. This helps water stream off while the glass is drying inside the foggy dishwasher. Or fill a large plastic bowl with white vinegar and give each glass a 15-minute bath. Then rinse with running water and allow to air-dry.

To remove food-colouring stains left in glassware by the dyes in powdered soft drink mixes and other beverages, fill the glass with a solution of 2 tablespoons of household ammonia in 1 litre of hot water. Let it stand for 30 minutes and then rinse with clean, cool water.

Hand-washing is best for fine glassware, even if you would prefer to use the dishwasher. To avoid scratching the glasses, remove rings, watches and bracelets, especially those with diamonds. Swing the tap head out of the way, so there will be no chance that you will accidentally smack any precious items against it.

Using both hands, clean one piece at a time in hot, soapy water. Gently wash with a soft cotton cloth or clean sponge. For stubborn dirt, scrub gently with a soft toothbrush. Rinse twice, first in a sink full of tepid water with a capful of vinegar mixed in and finally under a gentle shower of tepid water from the tap.

To clean really fine glassware Wearing gloves, use a solution of equal parts of methylated spirits and water, then add a few drops of ammonia. Water and the ammonia do the cleaning, while the spirit helps the glass to dry up very quickly. Apply the solution with cotton wool. Don't use this technique on glass with decorative gilt, as it could lift it off.

Crystal

Never put crystal in the dishwasher. Crystal is too fragile and soft for the dual action of dishwasher and detergent, which can etch and dull its surface. To preserve the special sparkle of crystal, always hand-wash it in sudsy washing-up water – unless it has silver or gold gilt, in which case you should use only plain, warm water.

To wash crystal, line the bottom of the sink with a doubled-up towel and fill the sink with warm water – not hot – and add two or three drops of washing-up liquid. Wash one item at a time. Grasp glasses by the bowl, not the stem, and wash gently. Pump the glass up and down in warm water to rinse. Dry upside down on a lint-free cotton towel or plastic dish rack. Better yet, put clean thick gloves or cotton socks over your hands and dry the crystal immediately with an old linen towel. This way, you'll leave no fingerprints or watermarks.

To remove stains, try the three-pronged approach:
• First, mix a paste of lemon juice and baking powder and rub gently on the crystal with a sponge, then wash and dry. Baking powder is about as abrasive as you can get with crystal without risking damage: bicarbonate of soda, which is coarser, is too much.
• Tougher stains can be 'riced'. Put 2 teaspoons of uncooked rice into the crystal piece, add water, and swirl. Repeat, if necessary.
• For stubborn stains, fill the crystal receptacle with warm water and drop in a denture tablet.

Here are some more crystal-cleaning tricks worth considering:
• For extra shine, add white vinegar or lemon juice to the rinse water.
• To wash the grooves of cut crystal, dip a frayed toothbrush into vinegar, lemon juice or soapy water and scrub.

Cookware

Cast iron and copper pans should not be put into the dishwasher. Most manufacturers also advise against washing them in the dishwasher where hot-water spouts and spray rinses are harsher than soapy water in the sink. And dishwasher detergents generally rely on alkaline-heavy cleaners to cut grease and extremely alkaline cleaners can mar cookware just as badly as acidic cleaners can.

Hand-wash pots and saucepans that can't be put in the dishwasher much as you would dishes. Scrape out any food residue with a wooden spoon or rubber spatula. Fill the sink with moderately hot water and add a squirt of washing-up liquid. As soon as the pot has cooled sufficiently, slide it into the soapy water and let it sit for a minute. Then gently scrub in a circular motion, using a sponge, brush or dishcloth.

Many non-stick surfaces – especially older ones – are easily scratched, so pay attention to the manufacturer's directions for cleaning. Clean the saucepan inside and out, sides and bottom. You will know that it has come clean when it feels smooth to the touch. Rinse in clean, hot water and dry with a kitchen towel.

Removing burned-on food can be done without working up a sweat – but you do need lots of patience, lots of hot water and washing-up liquid. Squirt some washing-up liquid into the pot or pan, fill it with hot water and leave it to soak for as long as possible. Nothing will remove burned-on food as a good two-hour soak in hot, soapy water.

Iron pots and pans

Cleaning well-seasoned iron cookware requires very little effort. Generally, all that's required is a little boiling water, light scraping with a wooden spoon and a quick wipe with a clean cloth. Dry thoroughly and lightly oil again.

For badly burned-on food, use a copper wool scouring pad. For extreme cases of burned-on food and grease, use any common oven cleaner according to the package directions. Rinse well. Then, unfortunately, you'll have to season the item as if it were new.

Store pots with the lids off to prevent condensation and keep your cookware clean, dry and oiled. A wire brush is best for removing rust. Really bad cases of rust may require the use of glasspaper or commercial rust removers.

Woks

A well-seasoned wok is practically non-stick and needs only light cleaning. Follow our instructions for seasoning and caring for your wok and it will last for ages.

To clean a new wok made of carbon steel (the authentic kind), begin by removing the temporary protective coating applied by the manufacturer. Scrub inside and out with washing-up liquid and steel wool and rinse with hot water. If some coating still remains, fill with water and boil until the coating dissolves. Empty the water and scrub again with steel wool and soap.

To clean a wok after cooking, wipe it out with a paper towel or damp cloth. Scrubbing a seasoned wok or using a detergent will ruin the carefully cultivated patina, but if you do need to scrub or wash with detergent, then simply re-season, as above. Similarly, if a wok gets rusty, just follow the steps for cleaning and seasoning a new wok.

To clean an electric wok, follow the manufacturer's directions, which will vary depending on the kind of surface and whether it is immersible in water.

Enamel pots and pans

Enamel is a baked-on coating for metals that doesn't rust or react with acids or chemicals and is usually easy to clean.

To clean enamelled surfaces, such as appliance surfaces, dissolve 2 tablespoons of bicarbonate of soda in 1 litre of warm water. Wipe the surfaces with a cloth or sponge dipped in the solution and rinse with fresh water on a clean cloth.

To clean enamelled cookware, let the pot cool first. Wash in hot water with washing-up liquid, rinse in running water and dry.

TO SEASON A NEW WOK

1 Set the wok on a burner and heat it until a few drops of water sprinkled into the wok do a mad dance. As it heats, the wok will change colour, becoming darker.

2 When it turns black, dip some wadded-up sheets of paper towel into sesame oil. Hold the wad in a pair of tongs and wipe the oil over the inside of the wok.

3 Turn the heat down to low and let the wok sit on it for 15 minutes. If the surface looks dry, wipe with another thin coat of oil.

4 Turn the heat off and let the wok cool.

5 Repeat the oiling and heating process once more before using the wok for cooking.

BURNT-ON FOOD

Despite your best efforts, one day you'll probably burn something onto your enamel cookware. Here's what to do.

Cover the stuck-on food with bicarbonate of soda and let the pan sit for several minutes while the powder absorbs the acids and oils. Then wash as usual. If the food still won't budge, add 1 litre of water and 2 teaspoons of bicarbonate of soda to the pan, simmer for 15 minutes and wash again.

Pots with metal or plastic handles may be washed in the dishwasher, but pots with wooden handles should not. Never use an abrasive cleaner or metal scouring pad. A plastic or nylon scourer is fine.

To care for enamelled cookware:
• Keep the cooking heat on low or medium except when boiling water.
• Never subject an empty pot to high heat.
• Use non-scratch wooden or plastic cooking tools.

Copper pots and pans

Unlacquered copper, found mostly on cookware, tarnishes easily but will brighten with elbow grease and the right technique.

To clean copper cookware, you should first be aware of the don'ts. Never use any scratchy cleaning tool on copper. And bleach will seriously discolour copper if it stands for a few hours or more.

Instead, try these natural methods:
• Sprinkle the item with salt and a little white vinegar.
• Cut a lemon in half, dip in salt, and rub.
• As long as the item can stand the heat, boil it in a large pan filled with water, 100ml white vinegar and 50g salt.

Always rinse with fresh water, dry well with a tea towel and buff with a soft cloth. If you want more shine, apply a commercial copper cleaner according to label directions.

Crevices can be tough to clean. These spots are also magnets for paste polish build-up. Use a cotton bud or natural horsehair brush and methylated spirits to banish the grime.

Swab small copper items with ketchup applied to a make-up sponge or cotton bud. You'll be surprised by how quickly they gleam.

Stainless steel pots and pans

Wash stainless steel pans in hot, soapy water or in a dishwasher. Scrub off stubborn food with a cloth, sponge or nylon-bristled brush, but avoid abrasives. If you're washing it in the dishwasher, be careful not to spill powdered dishwasher detergent on stainless steel – the strong powder will cause dark spots. To remove baked-on food, scrub with a paste of bicarbonate of soda and water.

Polish stainless steel with a clean, dry cloth.

To remove hard-water spots wipe with a cloth soaked in straight vinegar. Or use a stainless steel polishing product or Peek All-Purpose Metal Polish. Follow the label directions.

Cutting surfaces

The most effective way to keep cutting boards completely hygienic is to have several, so that you never mix one used for raw meat with a board on which you chop up cheese or fruit salad. But however many you have, don't skimp on the cleaning that is needed to kill the germs that build up on the board.

To wash a plastic cutting board, run it through a dishwasher, and the hot water and disinfecting ingredients found in dishwasher detergent will kill harmful bacteria. Wash your cutting board as soon as possible after each use, especially after preparing meat or poultry products.

To wash a wooden cutting board, it's best not to use a dishwasher because the dishwashing process may warp or loosen the glue that holds together laminated wood. Use a scrubbing brush to scrub the board by hand with washing-up liquid in hot water each time you use it. To kill germs, the water must be too hot for your hands to bear. So do it right and you'll have to wear rubber gloves. When done thoroughly, hand scrubbing is just as effective as a machine-washing.

To disinfect a cutting board, mix a teaspoon of bleach in a litre of water and apply it directly to the cutting surface with a scrubbing brush. Do not rinse. Instead, let the board air-dry to give the bleach a chance to work. If you need the board sooner than that, let it stand for at least one minute, and then pat it dry with a clean paper towel.

Butcher's blocks

To clean a butcher's block, use 10ml household bleach mixed with 2 litres of water in a bucket. Dip a small scrubbing brush in the chlorine water and scrub in hand-sized circles, taking care not to saturate the wood. When wood absorbs water, it swells. Then, when it dries out, the wood will crack, making a convenient trap for food, grime and germs. So brush the

butcher's block clean and quickly wipe away excess water with a hand towel.

As an alternative mix just enough salt into a few drops of lemon juice to make a paste. Rub it, with a cleaning cloth or sponge, hard enough onto the wood to free stuck-on or wedged-in food particles. Then rinse out the cloth or sponge and wipe the butcher's block clean. The result won't be as germ-free as cleaning with bleach, but it's a good, fresh-smelling alternative.

If the surface is oily or sticky even after a brisk scrub, you might need to get out the toolbox. Scrape up any build-up with a putty knife. Then gently attack the block with very fine glasspaper, graduating to finer grades, until you're satisfied. Then wipe clean with a damp cloth or sponge and season the block, as described in the panel left.

Items for storing and carrying food

We use a variety of containers to store and carry food. They need to be cleaned thoroughly after each use to ensure continuing hygiene.

Plastic containers

Nearly all plastic food containers are dishwasher safe. This includes the Tupperware brand. You can also hand-wash them in hot, soapy water, using a sponge or nylon-bristled brush to scrub away stuck-on food.

To remove stains on plastic containers, mix a paste of bicarbonate of soda and warm water and scrub with a nylon-bristled brush if the stain is light. For heavier stains, such as stubborn tomato, try one of the following techniques:

• Scrub with a solution of 60ml dishwasher detergent mixed with 250ml warm water. Rinse well. Wear gloves – dishwasher granules and powder are an irritant.
• Soak in a solution of 50ml bleach mixed with 1 litre of water. (Wash in soapy water afterward and rinse well.)

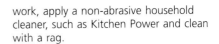

• Let the container stand in direct sunlight for a day or two.

Lunch boxes

To clean metal or hard plastic lunch boxes, wash with a clean sponge or cloth in hot water and a little washing-up liquid. Rinse and dry. Always do this after each day's use.

To clean soft-sided lunch boxes and bags, wipe the inside with a damp sponge or cloth. For spills, use a sponge dampened in hot, soapy water. Allow to air-dry thoroughly.

Cooler boxes

Ideally, you should clean your cooler after each use. The method for cleaning depends a lot on what you've had in it. Diet Cokes on ice? Easy. Just rinse it out with water. If you've had a full picnic, with meat and other foodstuffs, you're going to have to do a thorough clean.

To clean a large, rigid plastic cooler pour a couple of drops of washing-up liquid onto a sponge, then clean thoroughly. Swish out with clean water, and then turn the cooler upside down, so that the water drains out quickly.

To disinfect a cool box – if you've been carrying raw meat in it, for example – mix 5ml of bleach in a litre of water. Apply the solution to the cooler with a sponge or rag or pour it into a spray bottle, squirt it on and wipe. Then rinse with fresh water. Once your cooler is clean, let it air-dry with the lid open before you store it.

To remove stubborn food stains, make a paste by mixing bicarbonate of soda and water in a bowl. Dip a clean rag or sponge into the paste, rub the spot and rinse. If that doesn't

work, apply a non-abrasive household cleaner, such as Kitchen Power and clean with a rag.

To clean a soft-structure cooler, mix mild washing-up liquid in water and wipe the cooler down inside and out with a clean rag or sponge. Rinse and air-dry. Don't put it in the washing machine and don't use bleach on this type of cooler.

Thermos flasks

Clean after each use with hot, soapy water. Scrub them with a bottle brush, if possible. Rinse well and air-dry. Try not to

get water between the outer casing and the inner insulating flask.

For stubborn or hard-to-reach stains, fill the thermos with hot water, drop in two denture-cleaning tablets and let stand overnight. In the morning, rinse with clean water and air-dry.

If your thermos has an unpleasant odour that regular washing does not overcome, pour in a few tablespoons of vinegar or bicarbonate of soda. Fill the thermos the rest of the way with hot water and let it sit for half an hour. Then pour the solution out and rinse.

Table linen

Because of the food stains they so easily accumulate, most tablecloths and cloth napkins need to be, and are, machine washable. But simply throwing dirty or stained table linens into the machine may not be enough to keep them looking crisp and fresh under fine china, crystal and silver. A few tricks of the trade will help.

Wash table linens before stains set After a spillage or big, messy dinner parties, wash them in a washing machine as soon as possible, following the manufacturer's recommendations on the care label. Pre-treat stains with a commercial spot remover. For best results, don't let the pre-treatment dry before washing.

When ironing tablecloths, cut down on the creasing by placing a table next to your ironing board. Let the cloth hang over the table but don't let it drag on the floor.

If your table linens have lace trim, make sure the lace is machine washable. Some lace is not and may shrink considerably when washed in water.
• **If the lace is not washable,** have the item dry-cleaned.
• **If it is washable** – and most table linen lace is – wash it gently. The safest technique is to hand-wash it in warm water with a squirt or two of washing-up liquid.
• **If it is machine washable,** wash it in a net laundry bag tied at the top. This will prevent the lace from snagging.
• **To keep the lace from creasing,** which it will do in a tumble drier, air-dry it, laying it as flat as possible.
• **When ironing,** make small, gentle circular motions with your iron to avoid stretching the lace.

Bathrooms

Bathrooms are the places where we wash ourselves. For some people, they are also havens where they can relax away the stresses of the day. It goes without saying that the bathroom should gleam with cleanliness. But all too often they can harbour accumulations of mould and mildew, limescale deposits and a host of germs from the toilet. On the following pages, we tell you how to ensure that your bath, sink, shower and toilet are always sparkling and completely hygienic.

Baths & sinks

Wipe down the bath after each use with water and a cloth or sponge to keep soap scum under control. Staying on top of cleaning like this goes a long way, especially as most acrylic baths come with dire warnings about the danger of abrasive cleaners because their layer of acrylic is so thin.

And it's certainly true that if you scrub your way through the tub's protective finish, you'll soon have stains that are embedded in the glassfibre, porcelain or enamel.

Cleaning porcelain Most bathroom cleaners are safe. To polish stainless steel on fixtures, rub with bicarbonate of soda on a damp sponge. Rinse well with water.

Removing rust stains Squeeze lemon juice over the spot and use circular motion with an old toothbrush to gently rub the rust away. Be aware, however, that there may be permanent damage to your bath surface underneath, especially if the rust has been there for some time. Rinse with water and repeat if necessary.

Removing blue-green stains These are caused by water with a high copper content. Combine equal amounts of cream of tartar and bicarbonate of soda (usually a tablespoon of each is enough) and add some lemon juice drop by drop until you have a paste. Rub it into the stain with your

fingers or a soft cloth. Leave it for half an hour and rinse well with water. Repeat if necessary.

Cleaning an enamel bath Always check that your cleaning product specifically says it is 'safe for enamel'. If it doesn't don't use it. The problem isn't so much with new, super shiny enamel, but with enamel that has started to wear. Cleaning products hit on the weak spots, taking off the sheen from the surface. Stay with enamel-safe cleaners and you won't have a problem. Mousses work most quickly. So spray on, wait a while as instructed, then rinse off. For a good shiny finish, towel dry.

Cleaning acrylic tubs can be difficult because mild cleaners have little impact on a seriously soiled unit but abrasive cleaners applied with too much scrubbing pressure will quickly dull the finish. For everyday cleaning, spray on a bathroom cleaner that's designed for acrylic and wipe with a soft sponge. If the dirt and grime has reached the point where you have to be more aggressive, use a mildly abrasive cleaner, like Cif and a light-duty scrubbing sponge. Be sure to rinse well with water so that the chemicals won't stay on the surface.

WATCH OUT

When using any new cleaning product that you're unsure about, always test it first on an inconspicuous area to see that it doesn't cause damage to the material you are cleaning. And don't mix bathroom cleaners, in case you create a toxic stew with noxious gases. Mixing chlorine bleach with ammonia is particularly dangerous.

It's safe to use more than one type of cleaner as long as you rinse well between applications.

Showers

How can the shower – the place where you clean yourself – get so dirty? Soap, shampoo and dirt combine to make an unsightly scum.

To keep your shower enclosure sparkling, try these tips.

• **When you shower,** clean the shower straight afterwards. Steam from a hot shower will loosen grime and make the job easier.

• **With tiled shower walls and floor,** if you don't want to use a multi-purpose bathroom cleaner (the easiest option) you can use dishwasher detergent (either powder or liquid will do). Mix 60ml dishwasher detergent with 500ml warm water in a small pump spray bottle and shake to dissolve the detergent. Spray liberally on walls, let it sit for two or three hours and then scrub with a sponge. (Dishwasher detergent is an irritant, so wear gloves and don't get it on your skin.) Use a sponge mop to scrub high spots and the floor.

• **To clean tile grout,** make a paste of bicarbonate of soda and bleach (add bleach to the powder until it's a thick goo). Wear gloves and smear the paste on with a spatula. Air-dry for an hour and then scrub with a toothbrush and water. (Never use ammonia nearby, since ammonia and bleach don't mix.)

• **To prevent water spots,** rub the shower walls and doors with a squeegee immediately after you have taken your shower. Or try one of the daily shower cleaners. Mist surfaces right after you shower, while the walls are still warm and wet. The cleaner will prevent deposits from forming and will wash down the drain the next time you shower.

• **If your shower sprouts mould,** try this trick. Wipe down the walls with a solution of 1 teaspoon water softener, 1 tablespoon ammonia and 1 tablespoon vinegar in 200ml of warm water. Rinse with fresh water. Buff dry.

To clean shower doors, follow these pointers:

• **Wash them with white vinegar** to banish soap scum.

• **Or take leftover white wine** that's rapidly turning to vinegar, empty it into a trigger spray bottle and squirt it on your shower doors. Rinse well with water and dry with a soft cloth.

• **Wipe down the doors with fabric softener** on a damp cloth. Buff with a clean, dry cloth.

• **Another way to keep soap scum at bay** is to wipe down the shower doors with lemon oil. Baby oil works too, as does furniture polish, buffed with a soft cloth. (This also works on tiled showers, but don't put these slippery substances on a shower floor.)

• **Scrub shower door runners** with white toothpaste and an old toothbrush. Brush with vinegar to rinse. Or dip a stiff-bristled paintbrush in vinegar and scrub thoroughly.

• **To keep runners from growing mildew,** run the head of a small sponge paintbrush along the bottom runner channels when you've finished showering.

To remove soap film on a plastic shower curtain, place it in the washing machine with two or three large bath towels. Add 100ml of vinegar and wash, removing it before the spin cycle. Hang it up immediately to dry. If the mildew is out of control, use 180ml of chlorine bleach instead. To avoid a soapy build-up on the bottom of the shower curtain, rub it with baby oil. Always keep a shower curtain unfurled to give mould and mildew a less inviting place to grow.

GIVE YOUR SHOWERHEAD A BATH

Is your showerhead clogged with lime scale? If possible, unscrew the showerhead and soak it overnight in a bowl of white vinegar. In the morning, remove the deposits with a brush with moderately stiff bristles.

If you can't unscrew the showerhead, don't worry. Just pour the vinegar into a plastic bag, pull the bag up around the showerhead so that the showerhead is immersed in the vinegar and secure the bag to the showerhead's base with rubber bands or twist ties.

Toilets

Most people are not very efficient at cleaning toilets. And many are stumped by the stubborn rings that get left around the bowl.

To clean a toilet, work from the top down. Start with the tank, move to the seat, clean inside the bowl and then clean the base. Doing it this way will help you focus. Moreover, the dirtiest part of the toilet – and therefore the last place you want your rag to touch – is the base. For everything but the bowl, use a dry cloth and a spray-on bathroom cleaner. Spray the cleaner on the toilet surface and wipe it off with the cloth. Keeping the cloth dry makes it easier to wipe everything up. Wet it and you'll be chasing that moisture around and have to wring out the cloth, too. Avoid sponges, which work quite well but can absorb – and transfer – microorganisms.

Clean the bowl with a rounded bowl brush and cleaner. Avoid brushes with metal wire, since they may scratch the bowl. (For rings around the bowl see right.)

To clean around the hardware that holds the seat to the toilet and the toilet to the floor, use a grout brush or an old toothbrush.

RING AROUND THE BOWL

For stubborn rings around the toilet bowl, use a pumice stone, available at chemists, where it's sold to help you get hard skin off your feet. Keeping the stone wet, rub it on the ring until it's gone. This works for old rings as well. It will not scratch white vitreous china, which is what most toilets are made of, but it will scratch glassfibre, enamel, plastic and other materials. So don't try this technique if your toilet is made of any of these less durable materials.

Tiles

While they are two very different materials, ceramic and vinyl tiles are both low-maintenance, easy-to-clean surfaces. Both can scratch, so keeping them dirt-free reduces the risk of particles rubbing against the tiling and turning into a scratch.

For regular cleaning of floor tiles – both ceramic and vinyl – sweep with a broom or vacuum. Trapped dirt and sand are highly abrasive and can cause lasting damage to matt and glossy finishes. If you vacuum, avoid using the machine's beater bar, which can permanently damage tile finishes.

Once a week, clean floor tiles by going over them with a damp mop. Again, this goes for both ceramic and vinyl tiles. Damp mopping removes stubborn, smeared-on dirt. Never use excessive amounts of water with vinyl tiles, since the water can seep under the tiles and damage the glue. Avoid soapy or oily cleaners, as they can leave a dull film. If anything, add a splash of vinegar to the mop water. Or use a special tile floor cleaner, such as HG Shine Cleaner, sold at tile stores. Follow directions on the package.

For ceramic wall tiles, wipe them regularly with a damp sponge. As with floor tiles, avoid soapy or oily cleaners. Add a splash of vinegar to the water, or use a commercial bathroom cleaner. Never use abrasive scrubbers or cleaning products, such as scouring powders. These can scratch glazed tile, dulling the finish and making it more susceptible to dirt.

To keep grout clean, it's best to do it regularly so that scum and mildew don't have a chance to get a foothold in the porous surface. Indeed, it's a good idea to clean grout after you shower, while it's still steamy moist and the dirt has been loosened. Running the hottest water you can will kill germs. Get out of the shower first – hold the spray into the shower. You don't want to burn yourself. Then, to get things clean, mix together 60ml of vinegar with 3 litres of water and scrub the grout with a toothbrush or nylon scrub pad. For more cleaning power, go over it once with a degreaser, such as HG Grout Cleaner, from tile shops, which will loosen the germ-harbouring soap scum, then rinse.

Let your cleaning products do the work for you. Too much scrubbing will grind the grime in more deeply. Spray or wipe each product on and let it stand for several seconds. Wipe it down with a clean, wet sponge to rinse off the cleaning solution. If you must scrub, use a long-bristled brush that is not too stiff (you don't want to wear down the grout) or use an old toothbrush. Steel wool is too abrasive.

Medicine cabinets

You should do an annual review of the contents of the medicine cabinet to get rid of expired prescriptions, leftover antibiotics, old cough syrup and sterile gauze in broken packages.

Begin your review of medicines by checking the expiry date on each bottle or package and inspecting the contents for signs of deterioration. Pour expired liquids down the drain and throw expired pills straight into the rubbish bin to keep them out of the mouths of children and pets. If you can't find an expiry date, it is probaby old enough to retire. At the least, expired medicines are ineffective. At worst, formulations that have degraded over time can create new problems when ingested. So when in doubt, throw it out.

Developing an annual clean-out habit works best if it's tied to some other event, such as spring cleaning.

Cleaning the medicine cabinet itself is simple. Use a sponge and mixture of mild washing-up liquid in warm water to clean the interior and shelves. Or remove the shelves and put them in the top rack of your dishwasher.

Mirrors

For a crisp and bright reflection a variety of low-cost cleaning methods will produce sparkling results.

When using glass cleaner on a mirror, make sure you spray the glass cleaner on a lint-free cotton cloth or rag rather than directly on the mirror's surface. Not only do you use less cleaner, but you also prevent excess cleaner from running down the mirror's edges, where it can cause the mirror's silver backing to oxidise, turn black and brittle and eventually flake.

Old newspapers can do a good job of cleaning glass. Wear rubber gloves if you choose this method, to keep the printer's ink off your hands. Begin by mixing equal

amounts of vinegar and water in a bowl. Crumple the newspaper into a ball, dip it into the mixture and thoroughly wipe the mirror. Follow by rubbing with a dry newspaper or cotton cloth, to eliminate streaking. For extra shine after the mirror is dry, wipe it with a clean blackboard eraser.

To remove caked-on hair spray, wipe it off with a little surgical spirit on a soft cloth.

Taps

Most bathroom taps, showerheads, and metal shower frames are chrome-plated. Since chrome is usually plated onto another metal, be gentle when you clean it or you can scrub it right off. And don't get abrasive with chrome. Cleaners with 'scratch' in them can indelibly mar the surface.

When cleaning chrome taps

1 Rub a chrome surface with half a lemon dipped lightly in salt. Or use white vinegar

and salt on a soft cloth. Rinse well with water and buff to brilliance with a dry cloth or paper towel.

2 For chrome trim on taps and kitchen appliances, apply baby oil with a soft cloth and polish to restore lustre. If hard water has left deposits on taps, use a product like Flash Bathroom Spray, which will help to shift limescale.

3 To rid chrome of rust spots, crumple foil into a wad and rub hard on the shiny side. This technique also works wonders on golf club shafts.

Getting rid of limescale

Place a plastic bag in the sink as a liner and to catch any drips. Wrap a paper towel that has been soaked in liquid descaler around it and leave it for as long as the instructions advise. Natural alternatives are half a lemon pushed onto the edge of the tap or a paper towel soaked in while vinegar.

Cleaning gold taps

Polish them gently with a microfibre cloth. If the manufacturer allows, use a specialist metal polish to deal with scratches.

Living rooms

Dust is probably the biggest bugbear in most living rooms. The sheer quantity of objects that we keep there and the items themselves: books, ornaments and pictures, and electronic equipment all of which can be major dust attractors. The living room is also the place in your home which probably has the most variety in materials and textures, some of which may have been a major investment, particularly curtains and upholstery. Keep them clean and dust-free and they'll look good and last for far longer.

Blinds

Blinds – and especially venetian blinds – can act like miniature dust-collecting shelves. So make giving them a thorough clean and dust a regular part of your routine.

Dusting blinds Use the brush attachment on your vacuum cleaner and adjust the blinds to expose the flat surface. Then, from top to bottom and left to right, vacuum the entire surface. Reverse the slats and repeat.
Other options:
• Use a lamb's wool duster to gently clean the slats.
• Rub an old paintbrush along each slat.
• Wear an old pair of thick absorbent cloth gloves and wipe the slats by hand. Lakeland (**www.lakelandlimited.co.uk**) sells a Venetian blind duster, that is specially angled so you can move up and through the slats with speed.

Blinds made of natural materials can be damaged by water.
• **Parchment, paper or rice paper** should not get wet at all. Clean them as you would non-washable wallpaper – with commercial cleaning putty or an art gum eraser. Or find a spot remover that claims to work on the material at hand and test it on an inconspicuous area first.
• **Wood and bamboo blinds** should not be immersed in water. Wipe them down with a damp rag soaked in a solution of washing-up liquid and water. Then dry them quickly with a fresh rag.

Washing aluminium and vinyl blinds is fine, but don't use harsh cleaners or abrasives on them. And don't use any cleaner with ammonia on aluminium, because it will damage the finish. To clean aluminium or plastic blinds, you have a couple of choices. You can wash them where they hang, using water and a squirt of washing-up liquid, then rinsing off afterwards, or you can take them down and wash them in the shower or tub.

To give blinds a bath raise them, unlock the brackets at the top and remove them from the holder. Run enough warm water in the tub to cover the blinds and add around 100ml of washing-up liquid. Protecting your hands with rubber gloves, place the blinds in the water and extend them. Dip the blinds several times to loosen grime. Then let them soak for five minutes. Use your gloved fingers to clean both sides of each slat. Drain the dirty water and either rinse the blinds in a fresh tub of water or give them a spray under the shower, if you have a showerhead over the bath. Spread out the blinds on a clean towel and blot with another towel. When the blinds are completely dry, wipe fabric softener sheets, such as Bounce, on each slat. This will keep them from attracting dust, hair, insects and other grime.

Curtains

Dust your curtains once a month or so as part of a regular household clean. Use the upholstery tool on the vacuum cleaner or, if you can't get on with lifting this up high, a feather duster.

Clean your curtains about once a year. Look for the manufacturer's cleaning recommendations or, if they are homemade, ensure you keep the cleaning instructions that come with your fabric. Depending on the material, you will either machine-wash, hand-wash, or dry-clean.

If curtains can be machine-washed, use the delicate cycle. They may look sturdy and stable, but being continually exposed to the sun can weaken curtains by breaking down the fibres in the material. So the minute you wash them, they may begin to deteriorate. In the same way, be gentle when drying curtains in a machine. Take them out very promptly to reduce creases.

High heat can set creases in the fabric, especially when the cycle ends abruptly, leaving the curtains in a ball. An alternative to tumbling curtains until they are dry is to remove them from the dryer and hang them while they are still damp. This will reduce creasing and may help you avoid ironing them. If your curtains are not very dirty, you can skip the washing altogether and freshen them by tumbling them in a dryer using no heat.

Cushions

Keeping cushions clean is more than a matter of appearance. Dust mites, which can trigger allergies, often lurk within the folds of a dirty sofa. By removing dust regularly, you not only keep your cushions looking fresh, but you will also improve the quality of the air in your home.

To remove dust clean cushions about once a month using a vacuum cleaner with the appropriate attachments, such as an upholstery brush and a crevice tool. To avoid sucking out the feathers, test a spot of any down-filled cushion. If you pull out feathers, you will have to restrict your cleaning to gently brushing off the dust.

To give a more thorough cleaning, or to remove stains, wash your cushions. Generally, you should do this in situ, without taking out the cushion pad. The exception, of course, is if you're fortunate enough to have machine washable cushions. First, check the upholstery manufacturer's suggestions, usually tagged

to upholstery fabric. This tag will tell you whether you should use a water-based shampoo, a dry-cleaning solvent or neither of the two. Pick an inconspicuous spot on the cushion and pretest whatever cleaning technique is recommended. If there is shrinking or bleeding or running of colours, contact a professional cleaner. If not, carry on. Even if you can use shampoo, use as little moisture as possible. You do not want to wet the stuffing, because it dries very slowly and can make conditions even more suitable for moisture-loving dust mites. The trick is to clean using suds only.

• **The easiest solution** is to use a foaming carpet shampoo in an aerosol can. Follow the directions on the can, which typically tell you to allow the foam to stand until dry and then vacuum it off.

• **To make your own shampoo,** mix a squirt of washing-up liquid with a litre of warm water. Make suds by squeezing a sponge in the solution. Scoop the suds off the top and apply them sparingly with a sponge to the cushion surface. Rub gently in the direction of the fabric's grain. Rather than letting them dry as you would a shop-bought upholstery shampoo, work on a small area at a time, lightly rinsing each area as you go with a clean, damp sponge. Again, avoid soaking the fabric. Be sure to remove all the suds, or the residue will cause the fabric to soil faster.

If the fabric is dry-clean only and you just want to clean a stain, you can do it yourself, using a commercial dry-cleaning solvent such as Spotless, on sale at supermarkets. Don't pour the solvent onto the stain. Instead, moisten a clean white cloth with the solvent and use the cloth to draw the stain out. Blot repeatedly – never rub. Rubbing can stretch or damage the texture of the fabric. Always use solvents sparingly and in a well-ventilated area. And don't use solvents on cushions filled with latex foam rubber padding, because the solvent can dissolve the padding. However, if you need to clean the entire surface of a dry-clean only cushion, have it professionally cleaned.

Chandeliers

It's only when they are sparkling clean that the best chandeliers can be told apart from cheap imitations. You can buy the finest crystal in the world, but if it gets dirty, it's indistinguishable from cheap crystal. So if you are fortunate enough to have a fine example, clean it up and show it off.

A chandelier should be cleaned whenever it looks dusty, milky or cloudy. There are several methods to restore a chandelier's dazzle, depending on how dingy it has become. But if you maintain it regularly – say, a couple of times a year – you probably won't have to remove all the crystals and wash them by hand.

If the chandelier is not too dirty set up a stepladder in one or two spots where you can easily reach the chandelier without stretching and use one of these two methods to clean the crystals:

1 Make sure the switch is off, then lightly dampen a chamois cloth with a little water and wipe down each crystal while it is still attached to the chandelier frame. To clean the chandelier frame itself, wipe it gently with a dry cloth.

2 The two-glove method is also popular. Buy a pair of white cotton gloves, available in supermarkets and DIY stores, and dampen one glove with a glass cleaner, such as Windolene. Spray the cleaner onto the glove – never directly onto the chandelier – massage each crystal with the damp glove and then wipe it immediately with the dry glove.

If a chandelier is really dirty, you'll have to take down the crystals and wash them by hand – there are no dishwasher shortcuts. Start by climbing your stepladder and removing the bulbs and setting them aside. Then carefully remove the crystals. Run warm water in a bowl until it's about a quarter full. Add 30ml of white vinegar and 1 drop of washing-up liquid. The combination will remove any grease or residue on the glass but will minimise the amount of suds created, which are hard to rinse off.

Place a folded towel in the bottom of the sink – you don't want to break a crystal if it slips through your grasp. Wipe each crystal with your hands, then individually rinse each one under running water and dry with a soft cloth. If you don't dry them properly you'll end up with unsightly water spots.

Finally, wipe the light bulbs with a damp sponge, dry them with a cloth and return them to their sockets.

Cassette players

If you have a cassette player – be it at home or in the car – it may be losing its highs and lows. The audio problem may be caused by dust and grime combined with the oxide build-up that occurs when a tape moves through the player. You can improve the sound by cleaning the tape path.

To clean the tape path, you need to wipe over everything that the tape touches as it's played – the heads, tape guides, chrome pin and black rubber roller. Saturate three to four cotton buds with methylated spirits and thoroughly swab each area. The chrome heads should be wiped both vertically and horizontally. Keep cleaning until the final cotton swab comes away with no brown residue. Don't worry about black residue from the roller – that is from the rubber.

You can also buy cassette cleaning tapes, which generally don't clean as thoroughly as the cotton swab method but are a good alternative if you lack the careful finger work to get right into the tape deck.

To extend the life of cassettes, store them properly. Keep them out of extreme heat (that includes the back seat of your car or the dashboard in summer) and away from direct sunlight. Store them in their cases in the car's central console. Clean the player after every 75 hours or so of use and at least twice that often if some of your tapes are of poor quality.

CD players & CDs

When your CDs start skipping or the disc won't spin, there's a good chance the player's laser lens needs a quick shine. A clean machine will give a better sound, and regular maintenance will mean you won't miss a beat.

Cleaning the laser lens is inexpensive and simple on top-loading players and portable units. Front-loading players and carousel units require removing the player's cover

and finding the lens. Often there are too many mechanisms in the way, and extensive disassembling should be left to the professionals. In those cases, you can attempt to clean the lens with a cleaning disc, available for under £5 at CD shops and on the internet.

The disc looks like a CD, but its shiny side has tiny brushes on it and as the disc spins it brushes the lens. However, the lens has to be able to 'see' before the disc can spin, so a really dusty laser lens often won't respond when a cleaning disc is inserted.

But if your player's laser is in plain view in a top-loading model, even the most inexperienced home mechanic can clean it. Before you begin, unplug the CD player. If it's battery-powered, make sure the unit is off. Then do the following:

1 Locate the laser lens, which is a round glass bubble about a quarter-inch in diameter. The slightest bit of dust can prevent the laser from 'reading' the CD.

2 Dip a cotton swab in methylated spirits and, wearing plastic gloves, squeeze out the excess into a paper towel so it doesn't drip onto the CD player.

3 Using a circular motion, gently rub the lens for 5 to 10 seconds. The lens will move a little, but that's not a problem.

4 Let it dry. Depending on how much alcohol was left on the lens, it will take 10 to 20 minutes to dry. The CD player won't turn until it has dried out sufficiently.

Cleaning your CDs from time to time is also important, not only so that they play without distortion but also to prevent dust on the CDs from clogging up the player's works. The quickest way is simply to use

CD wipes – at around £3 for 12. But if you prefer, you can use a CD cleaning cloth or just about any lint free soft cloth moistened with a little methylated spirits. Hold the CD by its outer edge in one hand while cleaning with the other. Wipe it from the centre to the outer edge, as though you were wiping the spokes of a wheel from hub to rim.

Proper storage of your CDs will go a long way toward extending their playing time. Store them in their cases, and inspect them periodically for dust and fingerprints, which can cause a tracking error. Keep your player and CDs out of direct sunlight.

One last tip If the player is brought directly from a cold location to a warm one, moisture may condense on the lens, which will prevent the unit from playing. If this happens, remove the CD and wait about an hour for the moisture to evaporate.

DVD players

The more mechanical parts your DVD player has, the more likely it is to accumulate dirt and dust. Portable models are even more susceptible. Dirty discs or lenses can lead to mistracking, skipping, irregular speed and poor reproduction quality. Clean your player carefully if any of the above is happening.

Keeping discs clean is the first step in maintaining a DVD player, because they can carry dirt into the player's interior. Always hold them by the edges. Rid discs of dust with a shot of compressed air. Then wipe with a soft, dry cloth, starting at the centre of the disc and moving out to the edge. Don't use solvents or household cleaners. Always store a disc in its case to keep it dirt-free and keep discs out of direct sunlight and away from heat sources.

Cleaning the player's lens is the next step. Don't open anything that requires a screwdriver. Most warranties become void if you open the casing. Instead, press the button to open the mechanical drawer where the DVD sits. Spray a gentle blast of compressed air inside the opening to force out any dust or lint. It's not a bad idea to

spray the disc tray, too. Be careful to hold the can perfectly level to avoid getting any liquid near the DVD player. And don't hold the can any closer to the player than the distance recommended on the can – generally at least 10cm away. For less power, take your can further away from the player before you aim.

You can buy special lens-cleaning discs that will keep the laser lens good as new. Just open the drawer that holds the DVDs and place the cleaning disc in the tray. When you close the tray and hit Play, the cleaning action begins. Some cleaning discs, such as Maxell's, use an angular brush made of ultra fine synthetic fibres containing copper. Such discs not only clean the DVD player's lens, but also dissipate static that will attract dust.

To clean a player's exterior, a simple wipe-down with a soft, dry cloth is usually all that's needed. If the cabinet is extremely dirty, mix some washing-up liquid in water and get your cleaning cloth just barely damp before wiping it down. Avoid cleaning solvents (for example, alcohol), since they could damage the casing.

Televisions

Dust is likely to be your biggest challenge when cleaning your television. However often you clean, it seems always to come back, even thicker and more static.

Always unplug the television before you clean it, particularly if you need to use a wet cleaner.

To clean a TV screen, first identify the type of screen you have. Only standard tubes and plasma screens can be wiped with a wet cleaner as described below for the TV casing. Liquid crystal display screens, which include not only LCD TVs but also projection TVs with digital light processing (DLP) screens, should be wiped clean with a dry, clean cotton cloth. Consult your owner's manual. If the TV came with a cleaning kit, use its cleaner and cloths.

To clean a TV's case – or a tube or plasma screen that allows liquid cleaner – slightly dampen a soft cotton cloth with your chosen cleaner. (Pick a non-fraying fabric to avoid having ragged ends catch in the ventilation slits.) Glass cleaner makes the best cleaner, because it evaporates quickly. Or use a solution of 1 part liquid fabric softener to 4 parts water as your cleaner. Wring out the cloth so it's barely damp, never dripping and wipe down the television. Never apply liquid cleaner directly to your screen or casing – the drips could damage the electronics. Buff the screen afterward with a dry cloth.

Some other ways to clean your TV:
• Simply wipe the screen with an electrostatic dust cloth.
• Dust the body of the box with a dry cloth, or clean it with a solution of 1 part

neutral-pH cleaner (such as liquid hand soap) to 3 parts water.

VCRs & videotapes

As with any electronic gear, the cleaner you keep your VCR, the better all the small parts will work – and the longer the piece of equipment will last. The insides rarely need cleaning if you keep the outside clean. The only interior part you need to keep clean is the playback head – but you can do that with a head-cleaning tape.

Clean the front panel with a soft cotton cloth and glass cleaner. (First, turn off the VCR.) Don't use paper towels as they can tear and shed lint. Don't spray the glass cleaner directly on the unit. Instead, spray it on the cloth and gently wipe the cloth on the panel. For sensitive areas, such as around the panel control knobs and buttons, dust with a small, dry paintbrush. Don't apply cleaner to these areas, since it could seep into the controls. This way, you won't accidentally change your control settings, either.

To clean the chassis of the VCR – that is, the sides and top – use a soft cloth either dry or lightly misted with glass cleaner. Don't wet the cloth, since any residue left on the chassis may collect dust and lead to corrosion. Never spray anything directly on the chassis. Wipe away from the vent holes (not toward them) to avoid pushing dust into the workings of the VCR.

Dust the back of the unit, where the cables plug in, with a dry paintbrush. Don't use cleaner around this sensitive area. If you must remove the cables to access the back, be forewarned: many units store information for user settings, clock and timers, and this memory can be lost when the unit is unplugged from the electrical outlet.

Wipe cables down with a cloth misted with the same cleaner you used on the panels. Be careful not to pull the cables out as you wipe.

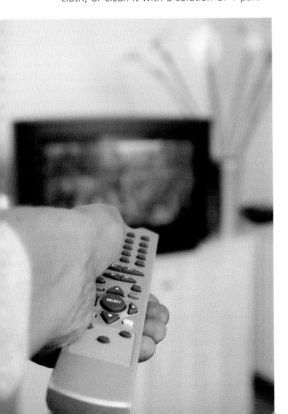

Clean the playback head periodically – once every few months, depending on use, or when the playback quality indicates a problem. If you rent a lot of videotapes, you may need to clean more often, since rental tapes bring with them dirt and debris picked up from all the other VCRs they've been played in.

Use a good-quality dry head-cleaning cassette – 'dry' because the liquid that sometimes comes with head-cleaning cassettes may not evaporate completely before another tape is inserted, which can worsen the situation by attracting grime from the tape to the playback head. Always read your owner's manual. If your VCR incorporates an automatic head-cleaning system, the manufacturer may recommend that you do not use any kind of head-cleaning tape.

If you need to clean a videotape's case, carefully wipe it with a damp cloth. Make sure you don't wet the tape itself or the tape path. Remove any labels or adhesives that are coming off. Loose labels that have fallen off are one of the biggest causes of tape jams.

Fireplaces

Ironically, fireplace cleaning is simpler during the wood-burning season and more of a project off-season. During the fire-burning season, cleaning will usually consist merely of removing some of the ashes periodically. The fireplace will actually work better when a thin layer of ash remains.

Many fireplaces have an ash pit, which is a receptacle underneath the area where you build a fire. If yours does, open it and push excess ashes into it. Or use an ash shovel to deposit the ashes in a metal bucket with a tight-fitting lid. Store the ashes outdoors in the tightly covered can for two days before final disposal, an important precaution as 'dead' ashes with live embers have started many a fire.

During the off-season, do a more thorough cleaning. Use a rubber eraser on any smoke streaks that have crept up the exterior of the fireplace. If your fireplace has warm-air

circulators, clean the ducts thoroughly with a vacuum cleaner.

You may also want to remove the black layer of creosote, a highly combustible residue created by burning wood, on the inside of the firebox. (The firebox is where you build your fire.) Remove the screen, irons and grate and sweep up all the ashes with a dustpan and brush.

Use a wire-bristled brush for the first attack on the creosote. If you want the firebox to be cleaner, use 50ml of soda crystals (from supermarkets) in 4 litres of water and apply it with a sponge. Brush with a stiff-fibre brush and rinse with clear water. Wear rubber gloves, since washing soda is caustic.

The off-season is also the time to have the chimney cleaned. This is a job for a professional chimney sweep, who will check the flue for leaves, bird's nests, cracks and soot build-up.

Clean the fireplace screen with a vacuum cleaner as part of your regular cleaning routine in the room. A screen catches more than the sparks that want to go flying into the room. It also catches a lot of dust. Periodically, give it a more substantial cleaning with soap and water. Pick a sunny day and work outside. Make a sudsy solution of warm water and a few squirts of washing-up liquid and scrub the screen with a stiff-bristled brush dipped in the solution. Then rinse it off with the garden hose. If you are working inside, rinse with a sponge dipped in clean water. Allow the screen to dry thoroughly. If it has brass parts, clean them with a brass polish.

Clean fireplace tools (shovels, pokers, tongs), as well as irons and grates, with the same brush and soapy solution. Use extra-fine (000) steel wool on rust or stubborn dirt. Dry the tools with a soft cloth. Give them a light coat of vegetable oil with a clean cloth; then wipe them dry with another cloth.

If rust is a problem on the screen or tools, you can renew the finish with a coat of high-temperature black spray paint, sold in hardware stores.

Clean glass fireplace doors with care. But there is one certain guideline: doors should be cleaned only when they're cool, never when they're hot. Common glass cleaners, such as Windolene, don't work very well on black creosote deposits. A solution of ammonia and water will clean them up, but the solution also may strip your doors of their heatproof coating. Instead, try this:

1 Dip a damp rag in ashes from the fireplace and rub the glass with that. Then wipe dry with a clean cloth. Or dip a cloth in white vinegar and wash. Dry with a piece of newspaper.

2 If you're still seeking perfection, try rubbing with white polishing compound from a car supplies shop.

3 Try a speciality cleaner, like those from the Stovax range, to shine up any glass doors or surrounds.

Furniture

If your furniture has an oiled finish, you should only dust and re-oil it. If it has a hard finishes – such as varnish or lacquer – you have more options.

Oil finish or a hard finish? Here's how to tell the difference. Put a few drops of boiled linseed oil on the wood and rub it in with your finger. If the wood absorbs the oil, you have an oil finish. If the boiled linseed oil beads up, you have a hard varnished or lacquered finish.

To clean oiled furniture, dust with a dry cloth. Don't use a dust-attracting product on the cloth and make sure the cloth is soft and free of buttons, zips and anything else that might scratch the wood. Then apply oil to the wood (boiled linseed oil, teak oil or

an oil recommended by the furniture's manufacturer). Rub the oil in with a clean cloth. Do this an average of once a month. If you have been neglectful, re-oil your furniture every two weeks for a couple of months to allow it to catch up on any oil that it has missed out on.

To protect oiled furniture, never put cloth items or water on it. Cloth items will absorb the moisture from the oil and dry out your furniture. Unfortunately, oil offers the least protection of any finish – get any water on it and it's spoiled – yet it requires the highest maintenance.

To clean varnished or lacquered furniture, dust first with a soft rag or stick duster. It's all right to add a little dust-attracting product, such as Pledge, to the rag or duster but not straight onto the furniture. Let it dry before you dust. If necessary, you can clean hard-finished furniture with a damp cloth and washing-up liquid. Now you're ready to polish.

To polish a hard finish, apply an aerosol furniture polish. First, mist the surface of the furniture and use one area of a rag to spread the polish, wiping in a circular motion. Turn the rag over and wipe off the excess polish. Avoid polishes that consist mostly of silicone and paraffin wax, because these tend to build-up and eventually soften or ruin a finish.

To give a hard finish a thorough cleaning and remove built-up wax, you'll need a few very soft rags. Soak one rag with white spirit. Wipe your furniture thoroughly,

flipping the rag frequently. Thoroughly go over all areas several times with the rag. Now dry the surface completely with a soft, dry rag. Repeat this process at least three times using a fresh rag.

Once the furniture is clean, you can polish. Spray the polish on the wood and rub it in with a rag, going in a circular motion. Now use another clean, soft rag – or flip the polishing rag to a dry spot – and wipe with the grain of the wood to remove excess polish. Carved wood should be cleaned in the same way, regularly with polish and once a year with white spirit. The only difference is that you'll need a soft toothbrush to get into the intricate details.

If a finish has become sticky, this usually means it has failed – the result of too much polish build-up, exposure to oils over the years, or the finish having degraded over time. Use white spirit and super-fine steel wool (0000) to remove the old finish, rubbing with the grain of the wood. Wipe three or four times with a rag and fresh white spirit. When you're done, the furniture will have to be refinished. Talk to a professional or follow the package directions on the finishing product you choose. Don't do this to a valuable antique. Take it to a professional.

To clean painted wood furniture, dust it with a water-dampened cloth. If necessary, use a mild, nonabrasive detergent (such as washing-up liquid) and warm water. Dip a rag into the cleaning solution and wring it nearly dry. Work on a small section of wood at a time. Rinse with clear water. Dry the surface with a clean cloth quickly before continuing.

Waxes and polishes are usually not needed on painted furniture, but if you do use a wax on a light-coloured painted piece, use a white, creamy type polish to avoid discoloration. Never use oil, oil polishes or oil-treated cloths on painted furniture.

A very old piece with its original finish should usually not be repainted or refinished, because you run the risk of ruining its value.

A NUTTY CURE FOR WATERMARKS

Is a white water spot ruining the finish on your dining room table? Peanut butter can be a surprising cure. Rub smooth peanut butter into the finish with a soft rag, over and over in a circular motion. If scratches appear, reapply, following the grain. The oils and abrasion from the peanuts will have a renewing effect on the finish. Next, take a dry cloth and wipe well. If the cleaned area now appears shinier than the rest of the surface, apply a little car wax with a mild cleaner in it, such as TurtleWax, to the spot. Then polish your furniture.

The peanut butter method works miracles, particularly with hazy-white water spots. Solid white water spots and the more severe black water spots probably require the attention of a professional restorer.

To make your own furniture cleaner for removing old polish and dirt, put 1 litre of water in a saucepan on the stove, add 2 tea bags and bring to a boil. Cool the solution to room temperature. Dip a soft cloth in the tea and wring the cloth until it's damp. Wipe, buff dry with a soft cloth and decide whether to polish it.

To make your own furniture polish, either:
• Mix 50ml of white vinegar and 150ml of olive oil.
• Mix 3 drops of lemon extract and 200ml of vegetable oil.
You can substitute baby oil for the olive or vegetable oil. Rub polish into the surface with a clean rag, using circular motions.

• Removing candle wax can cause further damage. Use ice directly on the wax to get it as cold as possible and immediately wipe up excess water. Once the wax is very cold, try carefully inserting a butter knife under the wax to see whether it will pop off. If this method doesn't work, don't attempt anything else. Consult a professional.

• Remove emulsion paint with water; remove gloss paint with white spirit. With a dry stain, saturate it in boiled linseed oil. After the paint softens, lift it off carefully with a putty knife. Alternatively, wipe with a cloth dampened in the boiled linseed oil.

• If a piece of paper is stuck to your wood furniture, dampen the paper thoroughly with salad cream, wait five minutes and rub along the grain with super-fine (0000) steel wool. Wipe dry.

Clocks

When cleaning wind-up clocks, what you don't do is as important as what you do. With any good mechanical clock, careful maintenance of the internal mechanism will prevent unnecessary wear and tear.

To take care of the inner workings entrust your clock to an expert. Clocks are too easy to damage if you do it yourself. Get the mechanism serviced every two to three years. Remember that time may be your worst enemy, but dirt in any timepiece comes in a close second.

Cleaning and oiling the inner workings of a clock is possible if you are careful. The first step is to wipe the inner workings with a dry, soft cloth to get rid of the worst of the dust and grime. Then apply special clock oil, which you can obtain at clock shops but not at hardware shops. It typically comes with a pen-like applicator. People often try using WD-40 first before they abandon the project and take the clock to a professional. Don't even try it. WD-40 is not a proper lubricant for clocks – it wears the mechanism out even faster, attracting dirt rather than repelling it. If you do clean and oil the clock yourself, use a clamp to hold down springs and other movable parts and don't put too much oil on the gears and the plate.

Cleaning the exterior of a wooden clock
Use a furniture oil to feed the wood –
lemon oil works well. To dust a clock case,
use a dust remover, such as Lemon Pledge,
sprayed onto a soft cloth, not on the clock
itself. Wipe the piece covering the face –
whether it is clear plastic, glass or acrylic –
with a clean, soft cloth. If you know the
cover is glass, use a window cleaner, such
as Windolene, but never spray it directly on
the clock. Spray it on the cloth and wipe
very gently, so that there is no chance of
excess liquid getting onto the clock face.

Glass furniture

Imagine you're cleaning a horizontal
mirror and you'll get the general idea
for cleaning glass-topped tables and
similar items.

Apply the cleaning solution – 1 part white
vinegar, 4 parts water from a spray bottle
directly onto your cloth, then rub into the
glass. Take care not to hold onto the table
as you clean, in order to avoid fingermarks.
   Apart from smearing, the other issue with
glass is breakage. So the most important
time for your glass furniture is not when
you clean it, but when you move it to clean
the carpet. Glass is heavy, so this may be a
two person job. Clean glass furniture as the
final stage of your room clean.

Knick-knacks

If you swoosh away the dust from your
glass menagerie or curios frequently,
it won't have a chance to turn to
greasy grime that will require a more
intrusive cleaning job.

To dust a whole rack of knick-knacks, use
a hair dryer or feather duster every couple
of days – if you prefer to 'swoosh'. Or wipe
them, one at a time, with a clean
microfibre cloth once a week. Either way,
you'll probably rarely need to wash them.

To wash knick-knacks, mix a little washing-
up liquid in warm water in a plastic bowl
and immerse china, glass, plastic or metal
objects. Use a clean, thick cotton sock,

worn over your hand, as a cleaning mitt. It
will get into most crevices. Use an old
toothbrush on places that your hand can't
get to. Rinse the items well with fresh
water and dry with a clean cloth.

To clean cloth items, try the vacuum
cleaner first, using the brush or crevice
attachment. If that isn't enough, put the
articles in a paper bag, add 2 tablespoons
of bicarbonate of soda, shake and then
shake some more. Remove the items from
the bag and brush or vacuum off.

Lamps

Cleaning your lamps doesn't make
them just look good, they will work
more effectively too: any dust on a
light makes it shine less brightly.

To remove dust from a lamp, use a
microfibre cloth regularly. The vacuum
cleaner with its brush attachment may work
better on some materials, such as unglazed
pottery or wood. The more often you dust,
the less often you'll have to do more
intensive cleaning.

Include the light bulb in your routine –
that's where the money-saving comes in.
Dust build-up reduces bulb efficiency,
wastes energy and raises your electricity bill.
To remove dirt, first unplug the lamp and
remove the shade and the bulb. Start with
a clean cloth or sponge dampened with
plain water. Wipe all parts of the lamp,
starting with the base and working up.
Don't wet the socket or the plug.

To avoid dulling the finish, buff the lamp
immediately with a clean, dry cloth. To
attack more stubborn dirt, try about
½ teaspoon of washing-up liquid applied
directly to a cloth or sponge. Wipe the dirty

areas, scrubbing gently if necessary. Rinse the cloth or sponge in clear water and go over the surface to remove the detergent. Follow with the dry cloth. Polish the lamp occasionally with a polish suitable for the material the lamp is made of.

To wash glass globes or chimneys, clean with a cloth or sponge and a solution of hot water and a little washing-up liquid. It's safe to immerse those parts as long as they don't have electrical connectors. Rinse with a solution of hot water and a dash of ammonia and wipe dry with a clean cloth.

Lamp shades

A lamp shade can set the mood in a room by directing and softening light. Whatever its colour or style, it will do this most effectively when it's clean.

To remove dust before it turns to grime, go over the surface – inside and out – with:
• a vacuum cleaner with the small brush attachment for sturdy cloth shades;
• a microfibre cloth for glass, plastic, paper, or metal shades;
• a soft-bristled horsehair paintbrush for silk, acetate and pleated shades.

To remove serious dirt, the safest cleaning method after dusting is to use a special sponge that's intended to be used dry. Ask for a dry-cleaning sponge at a hardware or DIY store. Use it like an eraser to rub away dirt. Try it on any shade, but be sure to use it instead of water on paper shades and those with glue.

To clean fabric shades that are stitched rather than glued, wash them in the bath. And while you are going to the trouble of doing one, it makes sense to do all your shades that need it. Metal and plastic shades can also be cleaned in the bath at the same time. To wash the shades, begin by drawing around 6cm of tepid water into the bath. Add 1 tablespoon of washing-up liquid and swish it around. Lay the shade on its side in the bath and gently roll it in the water. Metal and plastic shades can stand a little more vigorous cleaning, with a cloth or sponge. Change the water when it becomes dirty and wash again.
    To rinse, drain the wash water and draw clear water. Again, roll the shade in the water and change the water when it turns grey. Metal and plastic shades can be rinsed under running water and wiped dry.

To dry a cloth shade, use a towel to press out as much water as you can. Finish with a hair dryer, tipping the shade upside down frequently so that no water settles in the bottom of the shade, where it could leave a water stain. Drying quickly is important, because the metal parts of the shade can rust and stain the fabric.

To clean a glass shade, fill a sink with warm water and add 1 or 2 teaspoons of ammonia. Immerse the shade in the water and wash it with a cloth. Use a toothbrush to get into crevices. Rinse and dry with a clean cloth. White vinegar will also work.

Leather

Leather is any skin or hide that has been tanned. There are two main categories of leather requiring different cleaning techniques.

Natural leather has little surface protection and is susceptible to staining. It is not dyed with pigments, has no finish coat of polyurethane and is recognisable by its rustic, natural appearance. Even water or treatments suitable for other kinds of leather, such as saddle soap, may mar its surface.

Coated leather is recognisable by its pigment-dyed surface treated with a polyurethane coating. Most – but not all – leather garments, upholstery, purses and shoes are coated leather.

A few guidelines apply to both kinds:
• Follow cleaning directions from the manufacturer.
• Test any cleaning method on an inconspicuous area before using it generally.
• For any valuable leather article or serious cleaning problem, consult a professional, such as a dry-cleaner who specialises in cleaning leather.
• Avoid harsh cleaners and even excessive water, which can leave stains and remove dye and lubricants.
• Never dry wet leather near a heat source. To clean natural leather, rely on frequent dusting with a soft cloth. You could try removing dirt with an eraser, but even that might leave a smudge. There is little more you can do without making a problem worse.

To clean coated leathers, dust regularly with a cloth, occasionally with a dampened cloth. Wash every six months or so with saddle soap, which is available at tack shops, sporting goods stores, some shoe stores and hardware stores. Here's how:

1 Remove loose dirt with a stiff brush or damp cloth.

2 Rub a damp cloth on saddle soap and work up a lather.

3 Rub the soapy cloth on the leather using a circular motion and wipe away the excess with another damp cloth.

4 Allow to air-dry.

5 Buff with a clean, soft cloth.

6 Finish with a protective leather cream recommended by the manufacturer or a general-purpose one.

To treat spots on coated leathers, try these methods – but do patch test first:
• Apply unscented talcum powder to greasy spots and let it absorb the grease. Wipe off with a cloth.
• Rub with a cotton swab dipped in surgical spirit.
• Make a paste of equal parts lemon juice and cream of tartar, work it into the spot

(including scuff marks) with a cloth, let it sit for an hour or so and wipe clean.
• On mildew, use a 50-50 solution of methylated spirits and water on a cloth. Saddle soap also may work.

Light fixtures

How do insects and spiders manage to sneak into a ceiling light fixture that has no visible gaps? Whatever their secret, now and then you will want to remove their dried-out little bodies – and clean the fixture too.

To clean a wall or ceiling fixture, first turn off the switch and plant a sturdy stepladder nearby. Remove any grilles, shades, shields, globes, light bulbs or light tubes.

To wash the removable parts, fill the sink with hot water and add a little washing-up liquid. Lay a towel or rubber mat on the bottom of the sink to prevent damage. Immerse the pieces – except for the light bulbs or tubes – and clean with a soft cloth or sponge. Rinse and dry well with a soft cloth. Wipe the light bulbs or light tubes with a damp cloth, avoiding the ends that go into the sockets.

To wash the fixed parts, use a cloth or sponge dipped into the same cleaning solution and squeezed until it's barely damp. Wipe the fixture, being careful not to get any moisture in the socket or on the wiring. Rinse the sponge or cloth in clean water and wipe the fixture with it again. Wipe everything dry with another cloth and reassemble the fixture.

Rugs

The best way to keep a rug looking fresh is to keep it from getting dirty in the first place. Remove outdoor shoes when entering the house and you will cut down on 80 per cent of the dirt tracked inside.

Give rugs a good, regular shake outside. Vacuum them often, front and back, against the nap to pick up ground-in dirt. Rugs in high-traffic areas need a more thorough cleaning at least once a year; those in out-of-the-way places, less often.

To shampoo a small rug

1 Vacuum the rug.

2 Mix 100ml of mild washing-up liquid or rug shampoo with 2 litres of cool water in a clean bucket. (Don't use harsh detergents, sudsy ammonia, or regular ammonia on your rugs.)

3 With a long-bristled, soft brush or a firm, non-shedding sponge, brush the pile in the direction of the nap. Don't scrub. Wet thoroughly.

4 Wash the fringe of the rug, if it has one. If the floor under the rug is wood or otherwise easily damaged by water, place a plastic or rubber dust sheet under the

fringe. Then put a clean white towel on top of that (still beneath the fringe). Using a brush or sponge moistened (but not sopping) with the cleaning solution, brush the fringe from the knots out to the end. To rinse, replace the first towel under the fringe with a dry towel and blot the fringe with yet another towel dampened with warm water. Allow the fringe to dry on a third dry towel.

5 To rinse the main part of the rug, wet clean rags with warm water and press them against the rug.

6 Squeeze out excess moisture. (A window squeegee works well.) Squeegee the pile in the direction of the nap until no more water comes out. Use more towels to mop up any excess.

7 If there is plastic underneath the rug and it has become wet, replace it with dry plastic. Lay down dry towels and lay the rug flat on the towels to dry thoroughly on one side. Then turn it over to dry the other side, replacing the towels again if need be. Or dry the rug on top of a garden table in the shade outside.

8 If the pile feels stiff once it has completely dried, vacuum or brush it gently.

To remove a stain on a rug

Several important rules of thumb apply. Attack the stains in this order:

1 Blot stains, using clean cloths or absorbent white kitchen roll.

2 Scrape up whatever solids you can, using a kitchen knife, spatula or putty knife.

3 Work from the stain's outer edges to its centre. This is important, because doing it the other way round could spread the stain.

4 If the stain has penetrated the entire rug, place a clean cloth underneath the rug to absorb what seeped through.

5 Dilute the stain by blotting with a cloth dampened in clean water.

6 Try a carpet stain remover – Vanish or 1001 are both very effective.

7 If this doesn't work, mix 1 teaspoon of mild washing-up liquid with 250ml warm water. Blot with a white towel dampened with clear water. Don't saturate.

8 Shaving cream can also work wonders. Moisten the spot with water, work in the shaving cream and rinse with a clean cloth dampened with cool water.

9 Mix enough powdered laundry detergent with water to make a paste. Be sure the detergent has no brightening or whitening agents – choose one that's designed specially for colours like Ariel Colour. Let the paste sit for 10 minutes and remove any residue with a wooden spoon. Blot with a clean towel and rinse with another towel wrung out in warm water.

Sofa covers

Removable covers on your sofa are a fairly straightforward machine wash job (but check the care labels first). It's taking them off, then stretching them back on again that can be so time-consuming.

To remove dust and debris, give the covers a going-over while they're still on the furniture with your vacuum cleaner, using the upholstery attachment. For cushions, use the vacuum nozzle without any attachments.

To clean sofa covers, remove them and give them a good shake outside. Most can be washed, with the exception of rayon, which often requires dry cleaning. Consider washing curtains at the same time if they're made of the same fabric, so if they fade slightly, it will be consistent and not noticeable.

Covers will sometimes shrink the first time they're laundered, but it shouldn't be by very much. If hard to get out stains mean you decide to wash them twice, remember to put the curtains through a second time as well.

To dry sofa covers either hang over a drying rack or put them in a dryer. Some people feel that machine-drying is too harsh. If so, don't peg them out on the line: the wet weight of the cover is so great that it may pull the fabric out of shape. Instead, dry flat. Put some old dry sheeting on a garden table, then lay the slip cover on top, holding it down with a couple of books or bricks (wrapped in clear plastic) so that it doesn't blow off.

Put them back onto the sofa while they are still marginally damp. (Too dry and it will be impossible to fit them back on again.) Pull all seams and cording into place before you start. Save your hands and nails by using a wooden spoon to help tuck the corners of the cover back into place.

Upholstery

Upholstery poses a cleaning challenge, since it almost always covers some sort of padding – be it cotton batting or foam rubber – and because it is often not removable. Even when upholstery material can be removed from the padding, it is not always advisable to remove and wash it.

The danger with removing cushion covers from fixed upholstery is that they may not fit back on the cushions. There may also be some fading, which could make your sofa arms look very dark in contrast. Assuming that you are leaving everything in situ, the most basic aim with most upholstery cleaning is to clean without soaking the padding beneath.

Vacuum upholstery regularly to remove dust and dust mites. Use an upholstery attachment with a gentle brush end, so you don't damage the upholstery material. Use a crevice tool attachment for nooks and crannies. If your upholstered piece is stuffed with feathers, do not vacuum it unless it is lined with a down-proof ticking fabric. You might suck the feathers out. If you have no vacuum-cleaner attachments, brush the dust away with a soft-bristled brush at least once a month. Dust, when moistened or ground in, can stain upholstery.

For more thorough cleaning, or to remove stains, your upholstery will need washing. First, check the upholstery manufacturer's suggestions, usually tagged to your item. This tag will tell you whether you should use a water-based shampoo, a dry-cleaning solvent or neither of the two. Next, pick an inconspicuous spot on the upholstery and pretest whatever cleaning technique is recommended. If there is any shrinking,

bleeding or the colours run, contact a professional cleaner. If not, proceed.

If shampooing is safe, use as little moisture as possible. It is important not to wet the upholstery's stuffing, because it dries very slowly and can attract dust mites and mould. Clean using suds only. The easiest method is to use a foaming commercial shampoo in an aerosol can. Follow the directions on the can, which typically will tell you to allow the foam to stand until dry and then to vacuum it off.

To make your own upholstery shampoo, mix ½ teaspoon of washing-up liquid per 1 litre of warm water. Make suds by squeezing a sponge in the solution. Scoop the suds off the top, applying them sparingly with the sponge to the upholstery. Rub gently in the direction of the fabric's grain. Rather than letting the suds dry as you would with a commercial shampoo, work on a small area at a time, lightly rinsing each area as you go with a clean, damp sponge. Again, avoid soaking the fabric. Be sure to remove all the suds or the residue will cause the fabric to become dirty more quickly.

If the fabric calls for dry cleaning only and the upholstery is portable, have it professionally cleaned. If, however, you are cleaning a stain – or if the upholstery is part of a large piece of furniture – you can do it yourself, using a commercial dry-cleaning solvent. Don't pour the solvent on the stain. Instead, moisten a clean, white cloth with the solvent and use the cloth to draw the stain out. Blot repeatedly – never rub. Rubbing can stretch or damage the

UPHOLSTERY STAIN-REMOVAL BASICS

Here are some general tips for removing stains from upholstery:

1 Remove as much of the stain-causing material as you can by blotting with paper towels or scraping with a dull knife. When blotting up a large stain, always blot from the edge of the stain to the centre to contain it.

2 Avoid rubbing or pushing the stain deeper into the upholstery.

3 Since you never want to soak an upholstered cushion or piece of furniture, spray bottles are good for lightly applying water-based cleaning solutions and rinse water. You can buy one cheaply at a garden centre.

4 To dry upholstery that has been rinsed with water, lay a pad of paper towels on the spot and place a weight, such as a brick or a hardback book on the pad. (Put the brick or book in a plastic bag or on a piece of foil to prevent colour transfer to the upholstery.) Let the upholstery dry and then remove the towels.

texture of the fabric. Always use solvents sparingly and in a well-ventilated area. And don't use them on upholstery filled with latex foam rubber padding, because the solvent can dissolve the padding.

Vases

As well as looking awful, dirty vases reduce the lifespan of cut flowers. Residues, including algal growths, plugs up the stems and causes flowers to dry up more quickly.

The easiest way to clean vases is to scrub them with hot, soapy water and a bottle brush. Rinse well and let them dry completely before storing.

To remove white mineral deposit stains from the inside of vases, swirl a mixture of sea salt and vinegar around inside the vase. The salt will gently scour the surface while the vinegar breaks down the deposits.

Wicker, rattan & bamboo

Wicker is a term for something made of any of several materials that are bent and woven together. The most common types are rattan, cane, reed, bamboo, willow and twisted paper fibre (used in Lloyd Loom furniture).

Wicker comes in many finishes, ranging from natural to oil, varnish, shellac or paint. There are also synthetic versions of wicker made from resin, plastic or glassfibre. And when it comes to cleaning, the materials aren't all the same.

When cleaning synthetic wicker, you can be aggressive. This is the only wicker that should be allowed to remain outdoors. Clean it with a garden hose and plain water, using a cloth or sponge or scrub with a stiff brush and a solution of a little washing-up liquid in water. Rinse with the hose and dry with a clean cloth.

To clean natural-fibre wicker, keep furniture free of dirt with a vacuum cleaner, using the brush attachment. Other useful tools are a toothbrush, a stiff paintbrush and a pencil-sized dowel sharpened in a pencil sharpener. Wipe the wicker with a damp cloth or sponge, but undertake more extensive wet cleaning cautiously. Consult an expert before doing any major cleaning or refinishing of antique pieces. To find an expert, check with antiques dealers or on the internet.

To wash most natural-fibre wicker, use a solution of a little mild soap – Carex handwash, for example or a squirt of washing-up liquid – in warm water. Wipe with a cloth or sponge wrung out in the solution. Rinse with a garden hose and dry quickly – in the sun or with a hair dryer or fan. Don't sit on the furniture for two or three days, as you could stretch the fibres and cause them to sag.

There are some exceptions Don't hose down bamboo or twisted paper wicker. Clean these with a sponge dampened with soapy water, followed by a sponge moistened with clear water. Wipe dry.

To treat for dryness and cracking, use 1 part turpentine to 2 parts boiled linseed oil on natural-fibre wicker, except for bamboo. Apply with a paintbrush, using as much as the wicker will absorb. Wipe off any excess with a cloth and let it dry for three or four days. For bamboo, apply a thin coat of liquid or paste wax periodically.

Bedrooms

You spend around a third of your life in bed. That's a lot of time in the presence of potential allergens such as dust mites. So you will want to ensure that your bed, mattress and bedding are kept as clean and fresh as possible. As well as cleaning the heavier items described overleaf, change your bedding regularly – at least once a week – and wash sheets and duvet covers in the hottest wash that they can take. In the morning, air your bed for as long as possible before making it up again, to refresh it after the night.

Beds

Sometimes the biggest cleaning challenge is getting under the bed, rather than actually cleaning the divan or wood slats. It's worth doing both regularly, to increase the working life of your bed.

Wooden slats Clean these several times a year. Use the crevice tool on the vacuum cleaner to lift up dirt and dust from each slat. While doing this, take the opportunity to check the holding screws. They may need tightening to keep the base of the bed sufficiently supportive.

Wood headboards and support posts Use a cloth wrung out from a solution of sudsy washing-up liquid to remove grease and dirt. Rinse, dry and polish with a dry cloth (a microfibre one will give the best shine). Avoid using polishes as you'll smell the residue at night.

Fabric headboards You'll need to clean these grease and dust traps often. Get into the habit of giving the headboard a quick vacuum as you do the floor and you'll ward off the worst. But it's unlikely to be enough to keep the bright, fresh colour that attracted you to the headboard when new. So, in the morning, use upholstery cleaner and open the windows to air the room. Protect the mattress with a towel before

you spray on the cleaner. It's important not to get chemicals into the mattress, which could inhibit the action of the springs.

Divans Stick with vacuuming, unless it is particularly greasy. Try using a wrung out cloth, as above – but take care not to over-wet. If the divan is still dulled with grease, try to absorb particularly bad patches by rubbing in baby talcum powder, then brushing off with a stiff brush. Using a mattress protector and a valance will shield your divan from dirt. The highest risk time is the day that you change the bedding. If you remove the sheets, and want to put them back on later that day, take care not to use your uncovered bed as a dumping ground. And close the door if you have cats, unless you want a snagged base: an uncovered, undisturbed divan makes the world's most wonderful scratching post.

Mattresses & box springs

If you never give a thought to cleaning your mattress, here's a wake-up call: dust mites are almost certainly feasting on dander in your neglected bed and mould spores may also be multiplying.

Dust mites, tiny organisms that feed on microscopic flakes of dead skin, can cause allergic reactions in some people, particularly asthmatics. Washing sheets with hot water and occasionally vacuuming the mattress will help keep mites under control.

Periodic cleaning of a mattress will prolong its life even if you don't have allergies. Here's how:

1 Every six months, rotate the mattress end to end and vacuum the exposed surface. Run the brush attachment over the entire mattress, including the sides. This will removes dust mites and mould spores. Empty the vacuum cleaner bag or cylinder outdoors or throw it away.

2 Once a year, flip the mattress over and vacuum it. Remove the mattress and vacuum the box springs with the brush attachment. If you have the type of box springs with exposed springs, use a bottle brush to reach in and lift away dust.

Removing stains from a mattress can be tricky, because moisture can be very harmful. Clean with upholstery shampoo, following the package directions. Or lift the stains out using dry suds, made by whipping a grease-cutting washing-up liquid or detergent in water. Keep mixing until you have lots of suds. Using a clean cloth, soft brush or sponge dampened with warm water, apply the suds in a circular motion to the stain. Then draw out the moisture with a clean, dry towel. Repeat the procedure if necessary, then wipe with

a clean cloth dampened with clear water. Again, press a dry towel against the spot to draw out the moisture. The key is to leave as little water on the mattress as possible, because moisture in the mattress filling can lead to mildew and mould growth.

To speed drying, blow an electric fan toward the mattress or take the mattress outside and let the sun do the job. If you've cleaned the entire mattress (one small section at a time), you may want to use a dehumidifier in the bedroom to draw out even more moisture.

Pillows

Pillows can be a big source of sneezes – particularly for allergy sufferers. Dust, body oil, perspiration and dead skin particles gather on (and inside) pillows. That combination is bad enough, but pillows also harbour dust mites, microscopic organisms that many people are allergic to.

And if you have goose down, dust and dirt act as abrasives and shorten the life of the down. So give your pillows – which are usually stuffed with either a synthetic fibre, goose down or feathers – a good cleaning at least twice a year.

Most fibre-filled pillows can just be put in the washing machine. While you should always follow the instructions on the pillow's care tag, generally you can use the cold-water cycle for fibre-filled pillows and tumble them in the drier on low heat. Or you can dry it on a clothes line. Hang the pillow in the sun by one corner. Make sure it is completely dry before using.

Down and feather pillows should be machine-washed or dry-cleaned depending on the manufacturer's suggestion. Some recommend dry cleaning only, claiming that machine-washing down and feathers reduces their natural resilience. If you do decide to dry-clean your pillows, take them to a cleaner with experience of cleaning down. If there are any lingering dry-cleaning solvent fumes, air the pillows until they are all gone.

If you machine-wash down pillows, the big problem is drying them afterwards. Most are fine in the machine – as long as you have checked the care label – but it is not very safe to dry them in the tumble dryer as it could overheat. Also, it's expensive: it may take four hours of tumble drying to dry a pair of pillows. Waiting for a hot day and drying them outside is your best option. However, it's still such a lengthy chore, that you may simply prefer to give your pillows a fixed life, then throw them out and buy some brand new ones.

Sheets

Cleaning sheets is an easy job for the washing machine. Read the care labels on cotton and polyester-cotton sheets to find the maximum temperature of the wash.

For best results, wash as part of a mixed load: a pair of sheets plus two hand towels and flannels will fill most washing machines. When drying, to minimise (or hopefully avoid) ironing, remove the sheets when still just damp and fold into eighths.

Store in the airing cupboard. If you are doing a turnaround on a set of sheets, you will need to dry them fully and then iron.

Duvets

Check the care label before you start – and get out the bathroom scales at the same time. Many synthetic double duvets are washable, but they may weigh more than the capacity of your washing machine, which will mean a trip to the launderette.

Single, synthetic duvets shouldn't be a problem and are a simple machine wash and tumble dry job. Feather and down duvets are best professionally cleaned. In truth, it's not the washing that is the big problem – your feather duvet may indeed be up to machine washing. But the drying can be near impossible. It is no exaggeration to say that it can take several days to dry a quality feather duvet.

For this reason, when accidents happen – a child or pet wets the duvet or you spill coffee – it is best to restrict your washing to that section only.

Take the duvet to the bath and using a solution of hand-washing detergent in the sink or bath (which ever is more appropriate) immerse the soiled section only. Rinse with fresh water, then blot off as much water as you can by putting the duvet between two dry towels. Finish spot drying with a hair drier.

For urine or other related accidents, make sure that you get rid of all of the smell to avoid it becoming ingrained.

Blankets

It's a myth that you can't wash blankets, because they will shrink and distort. These days, most blankets, including some made of wool, can be washed at home.

Check the care labels and make certain that your washing machine and tumble dryer will hold the blanket comfortably. Weigh the blanket first, if you are unsure and check it against your machine's maximum weights. Don't just cram it in and go – the blanket won't rinse or dry properly if there isn't really enough room. In that instance, take your blanket to a self-service launderette with a commercial-size washing machine and tumble dryer.

Before washing a wool blanket, check the label to make sure it is washable. If it isn't, have it dry-cleaned. If you are going to wash it, measure the blanket and save the measurements for later – you may want these as a guide as to how far you want to stretch the fibres out to afterwards.

Pretreat any spots or stains with stain remover, following label directions. If the binding (the narrow fabric along the edges) is really filthy, use a nylon-bristled scrubbing brush to gently scrub it with washing-up liquid or make a paste of equal parts non-biological detergent and water and apply it carefully. Gentleness is critical here because the binding may shred if it's old and worn.

To machine-wash a wool blanket use a non-biological powder that's safe for wools and choose the gentle cycle, with a minimal spin. Most machines have a specific wool programme that you should choose.

To hand-wash a wool blanket – if your blanket won't fit into the machine, or you're worried that it will be too much – fill the bath with cold water and add 1 measure of a hand wash detergent that is suitable for wools, such as Woolite. Put the blanket in the tub and press down to wash.
    To rinse, fill the tub several times with fresh, cool water. Squeeze out, but don't wring, excess water by rolling up your blanket in two or three large white towels.

To dry a wool blanket you have several drying options:
• The first is to use your tumble dryer, but only if you have a 'No heat' setting.
• Or, spread out dry towels on a clean garden table, flatten the blanket and stretch it to its original shape.
• Hang the blanket over two tightly strung clothes lines that won't droop under its weight. If you chose the second or third approach, plump up the blanket afterward in the dryer on the 'No heat' setting.

To clean a cotton or acrylic blanket Simply wash as you would other cotton or acrylic items – in the washing machine, following the maximum temperature on the care label. Dry a knitted cotton blanket in a drier on low heat so it won't pill. For other cotton blankets, the regular setting is suitable. Or hang a cotton blanket from a taut clothesline to dry. Tumble-dry an acrylic blanket on low heat.

Bedspreads

Laundering a bedspread, particularly if it's large or padded, can be difficult at home. You may want to take your bedspread to a local launderette, where the washers and driers are bigger than most home varieties.

Before washing Check the care label to make sure that your bedspread is washable and weigh it to check that your washing machine will be able to deal with the load. Pre-treat any heavily soiled areas with a pre-wash product, such as Shout. Set the washing machine to a delicates programme with a normal spin cycle. Add the bedspread and detergent.

Drying a bedspread Transfer it to the drier. Add a couple of clean, dry towels and then

toss in several clean tennis balls that will knock against the spread to keep its filling from clumping. Stop the dryer twice to make sure it isn't getting too hot. Shake the bedspread out once, too, to make sure the padding doesn't jam up in one corner.

To fluff up a candlewick bedspread hang it outside on a clothesline in a stiff wind, with the knotted sides facing. The knots will perk up as they rub against one another. Or, once it is dry, spread it on a clean floor and sweep the surface with a clean broom.

Quilts

Old or handmade quilts need special care. Though beautiful, their age and character often appears in the form of water rings, dye bleeds, stains of unknown origin and tears – all of which will dictate how you wash it.

Test the fabric strength Depending on the quilt's age, some pieces of the fabric may deteriorate simply when touched. If you have such a weak patch, tack the area with needle and thread or consider replacing the patch altogether.

Test the dyes Each piece of fabric and each dye need to be tested for colourfastness. Mix 1 tablespoon each of ammonia and liquid laundry detergent per 3 tablespoons of water. Dampen a white towel with the solution. Touch – don't press – the damp cloth or towel to an obscure corner of the quilt. Leave it on for 30 seconds. Then lightly blot the spot with a dry part of the cloth. If there is no bleeding take another part of the quilt. Find a dry spot on the white cloth and dampen it in the solution. Press harder on the quilt and wait a minute before blotting. Finally, take another part of the quilt, press harder with the damp cloth and lightly rub. If your white cloth is still white or has picked up no more than a trace of the colour from the test spot, it's safe to wash your quilt.

The more colourfast your quilt, the warmer the water you can use, but don't go much warmer than tepid. If it has weak spots in the seams or fabric, put it in a mesh laundry bag and use a low or non spin programme.

Or use the bath Fill it with enough water to cover the quilt with 6–10cm to spare. Add detergent, choosing one that contains bleach if your quilt is yellowing. Swirl the water to mix. Then lay the quilt in the water, spreading it as much as possible. Stay by the bath-side for 10 minutes, swishing, smoothing and squeezing with your hands to release the dirt. If you notice that the colour is running, drain the bath and rinse the quilt with cold water.

When it's time to rinse, pull out the plug and push the quilt to the other end of the bath. Bunch it up until all the water has drained. Then squeeze the quilt to force out the excess water. Rinse by agitating the quilt as you did when washing. If the rinse water becomes discoloured, repeat the drain-and-rinse process. If you used bleach, rinse it twice. Squeeze the quilt again.

To dry the quilt, try tumbling it in the drier with cool air, if you think the quilt can stand it. If not, hang it on a clothesline.

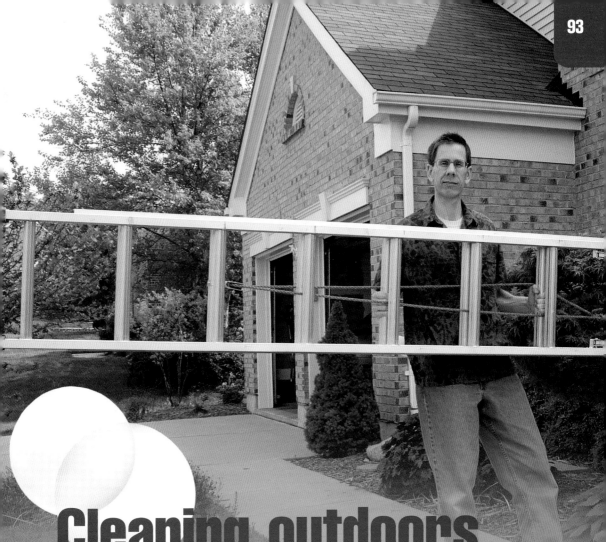

Cleaning outdoors

Keep your garden and the areas surrounding your house clean and tidy and you will make it a more pleasant place to spend time, be it gardening, playing games or simply relaxing when the weather is warm. Being warm and humid, your greenhouse can be a potent breeding ground for fungi and bacteria, so keep it clean and uncluttered and you will raise healthier plants. Items kept outdoors, including awnings, garden furniture, ornaments, barbecues, hoses and tools will also benefit from careful maintenance: they will last longer and be clean and ready to use when you need them.

Asphalt

Though asphalt is tough and hardwearing, there are a surprising number of cleaning considerations where the rubber meets the road.

To clean a driveway or other asphalt surface, give it a good wash once a year. Remove leaves and dirt with a broom or leaf blower. Mix 1 scoop (60ml) of detergent in a bucket with 4 litres of water. Splash some onto the driveway as needed for spot cleaning and scrub with a stiff broom. Then give it a good rinse with a garden hose. Avoid high-pressure hoses or steam washing, which could damage the asphalt.

Clean petrol and oil spills as quickly as possible. Asphalt is a petroleum-based material. This means a puddle of petrol or oil could eat a hole in your driveway. Soak up a spill with paper towels and spray away any of the remainder with a garden hose. For a little more cleaning power, mix detergent in water as described above and work at the spot with a stiff-bristled scrubbing brush. And next time, take preventive measures. Lay down some cardboard, newspaper or plastic when you add oil or petrol to your lawn mower or oil a bike chain on the drive.

To remove asphalt stains on clothing pretreat the stain with a biological stain removing product, then machine wash. If you get asphalt on your shoes, spray them with WD-40 and scrape the asphalt off with a paint scraper or putty knife. Make sure to rinse your shoes well before you wear them in the house.

Awnings & canopies

A dirty awning or canopy can mar the look of your whole house. Keeping it clean will also help it last a lot longer.

Most acrylic awnings have a soil and stain-resistant finish. Where necessary, use a stepladder to reach the awnings. Spot-wash by applying a solution of warm water and

mild washing-up liquid with a sponge. Rinse thoroughly with clean water and air-dry. For stubborn stains, use a fabric stain remover, following the directions on the container. Again, rinse well and air-dry.

Mildew on an acrylic awning is usually found growing on dirt, leaves and other materials that are not removed from the fabric. Acrylic awnings themselves do not promote the growth of mildew. To remove mildew, mix 50ml of bleach with a squirt of mild dishwashing liquid in 5 litres of water. Apply to the entire area and allow it to soak in (but not to dry). Scrub with a sponge. Rinse thoroughly and air-dry. Don't use bleach on any logos or prints that decorate the awning.

Cleaning vinyl or fabric awnings is usually done with spray cleaners that work best if you don't wet the awning before cleaning it – a garden furniture upholstery cleaner (from DIY stores) is fine. Stand on a stepladder so that you can evenly mist on your vinyl cleaner. Start from the bottom and work up. Before the cleaner dries, scrub the awning with a sponge or soft to medium-bristled brush. (Brushes work best on fabric awnings.) Never use abrasive cleaners or scrubbers. Rinse by spraying with a garden hose until the water runs off clear. You must remove all the cleaner, because leftover cleaner will leave a chalky film once it dries. Don't use a pressure washer to clean your awning. It's ineffective and can cause permanent damage.

Mildew on a vinyl or fabric awning can be removed using a solution of 50ml bleach per 5 litres of warm water. Before using the solution, however, test it by rubbing a solution-soaked cotton bud on a hidden section of awning to make sure it does not cause the colours to fade or run. Don't let the bleach solution dry on the awning. Rinse thoroughly with water.

Barbecues

Before you start the barbecue, make sure it's ready to cook with. A clean machine makes for tastier, healthier and safer meals.

Cleaning a barbecue Remove the grill grates and clean it inside and out with 2 parts hot water to 1 part washing-up liquid. (With gas barbecues, you'll need to cover the gas receptacles with aluminium foil to stop water leaking inside.) Scrub with a nylon brush to prevent scratching (or just a cloth, if you are concerned that even that might be too much), follow with a hot water rinse and towel dry. Finally, apply vegetable oil, using a clean cloth, to the barbecue's outside surface. This will keep the body of the barbecue shining and lubricated against the elements.

If the instructions say the racks are dishwasher safe you are lucky. If not, several methods work well. First scrub them with a wire brush and the hot water and washing-up liquid mix described above. If they are too encrusted, spray them with oven cleaner. Place the treated grates in a rubbish bag lined with paper towels, tie the top closed and stash the bag in the garden shed, out of reach of pets and children for a couple of hours or even overnight – powerful chemicals are at work. When you re-open the bag to remove the grates, point the opening away from your face to avoid inhaling potent fumes. Thoroughly hose off the grates, wipe them down with hot water and washing-up liquid and rinse.
 If you have a self-cleaning oven, your clean-up couldn't be easier. Just put the grill grates in the oven and let the intense heat do the work for you.

Cleaning a gas grill You need to take these additional cleaning and maintenance steps, ideally when you get the barbecue out after the winter.

1 Ensure the gas bottle is disconnected.

2 Inspect the burners for cracks and corrosion and replace if damaged.

3 Using a pipe cleaner or non-metallic bottle brush, clean the tubes, which carry gas to the burners. These tubes make an excellent hiding spot for spiders, whose nests can block the flow of gas and cause an explosion.

4 Check for leaks in the connector hose. Brush around the connections between the gas bottle, the regulator and the hose with soapy water and turn on the gas. If you smell gas or see bubbles, turn off the gas, tighten the connections and repeat the test. If it is still leaking – a potentially dangerous problem – you need a new hose.

Cleaning lava rocks Use a stiff-bristled brush or remove the rocks and clean them with a degreasing cleaner. One batch of lava rocks should see you through the whole summer, even if you are an enthusiast. Turn them over every third time you cook, to burn off the dripped grease. To cut down on mess try to eliminate some of the grease. When you've finished cooking, leave the burners turned on for 10 to 15 minutes with the cover closed. Let the grill cool and then scrape away the residue with a wire brush. This will be easier if you coat the grates with a non-stick cooking spray each time you cook.

Brick

Exposed interior brick can be cleaned by simply putting the brush attachment on your vacuum cleaner and running it over the wall. The brush will loosen the dust and dirt and the vacuum will suck it up.

On exterior brick, particularly in a damp and shady spot, mould, mildew and algae are often a problem. To kill and remove the growth, mix 50ml of bleach with 5 litres of water in a bucket. If you find you need

more strength, increase the bleach or try Thompsons Moss and Mould Killer. Wearing rubber gloves, dip a stiff-bristled brush (not metal) in the solution and scrub. To rinse, hose the brick down with fresh water.

For cleaning dingy brick some masonry specialists swear by caustic soda, an ingredient in powerful oven cleaners. Follow the instructions precisely and only apply if you can be sure that children or pets won't have access to the wall while it is coated with this extremely strong solvent.
  Oven cleaner is an expensive option if you have a large section of brickwork to wash. So just use the caustic soda – Starpax do one, on sale at DIY stores. Because it is so powerful (it will cause burns instantly) always fill the water bucket first, then add the caustic soda to the water. This minimises the risk of getting splashed. Wear rubber gloves, long sleeves and protective goggles. Apply the solution with an old rag. Let the cleaner sit for 15 minutes and follow up with a scrubbing brush. Apply the cleaner again if necessary and scrub once more. Rinse with water.

To brighten soot-stained brick try this old masonry trick. Mix a can of a cola soft drink (its acid adds cleaning power), 100ml of an economy all-purpose household cleaner, such as Tesco All Purpose Value Cleaner and 4 litres of water in a bucket. Sponge the solution onto the sooty brick and let it sit for 15 minutes. Scrub with a stiff-bristled brush to loosen the soot. Rinse with a clean sponge and fresh water. If you are working outside, use a hose. To make the solution more powerful, add more cola.

As an alternative, buy a commercial soot remover from a shop that sells fireplace equipment and use following the product's directions.

Concrete

Your first step is to work out what caused the stain and then act swiftly. The longer a stain is untreated, the more likely it is to seep in.

Clean concrete at least once a year. Protect adjacent glass, metal, wood, plants or other decorative materials with a tarpaulin or a large piece of old plastic. Test the method in an obscure spot to make sure it works. Never use a metallic brush on concrete, as metallic fibres can get trapped and rust.

• If concrete is old and crumbly, brush it lightly with a soft brush. If that doesn't work, move on to warm water and mild detergent, adding white vinegar to the water if soil and stains persist.
• Wet the concrete with warm water and scrub with a soft, non-metallic brush. Wash off the concrete with a garden hose fitted with a high-pressure nozzle and let it dry.
• If that isn't enough, add 1 measure of non-biological washing powder to a pail of warm water and scrub again.
• Or use a biological detergent, mixed with water and 20ml of ammonia, applied with a stiff nylon brush.
• Rent a pressure-washing machine to squirt off dirt that's not ground into the concrete.

To remove serious stains, such as tyre marks, grease, oil and other stubborn materials, you will have to get aggressive. For fresh grease stains, first sprinkle dry cement, cat litter or sand on the spot, letting it sit for an hour to absorb at least some of the grease. Then sweep it up with a broom and dustpan. For more difficult grease spots, use a commercial degreaser, following label instructions.

Decking

Your deck is an outdoor room – exposed to sun, wind, rain and ice. To keep it looking its best, you need to clean it well enough to maintain it for the long term. Even decks made of pressure-treated wood deteriorate unless they are cared for.

harm plants, oxygen bleach is relatively gentle and non-toxic. Simply apply it with a mop or brush. Don't scrub. Wait 15 or 20 minutes for it to soak in and then hose down the deck to remove the solution. If you use a wood sealer, such as Thompson's Water Seal, on your deck, you will need to reapply it after washing with oxygen bleach, which strips away sealers along with dirt and mildew.

Don't use a pressure washer. Pressure washers are expensive, dangerous and harmful to wood. The extreme water pressure will break up the wood fibres – exactly what you are trying to prevent – leaving the surface fuzzy, more susceptible to the weather and in poor condition for refinishing with stains and sealers. Only use them as a last resort and then be very careful. Use the lowest pressure setting available. Hold the nozzle at an angle at least 30cm away from the deck's surface.

Dustbins

Only putting items inside a dustbin that are themselves inside securely tied plastic bags will reduce the frequency with which you'll need to clean your dustbin. If you don't use sturdy sacks – or if you get a split – you should disinfect the bin each week, after it's been emptied by the council rubbish contractor.

Hosing out the bin is the easiest option, but if that's too much of a hassle for just one item, use an old watering can, marked clearly as not being suitable for watering flowers anymore. You can direct the flow of water needed to clean more easily than simply pouring it in from a bucket.
  First, take your dustbin to an outside drain: you won't want to tip foul-smelling water onto your drive or flower-beds. Fill the watering can with a mix of 40ml bleach to 5 litres of water and use this to rinse around the bottom and side of the bin. Empty down the drain and repeat.

Wash the lid with the same solution, then invert both to dry. Later that day, when you next need to put a sack out in the dustbin, you can put your clean bin back together again.

Sweep regularly to keep your deck free of leaves and twigs. Otherwise, pollen and twig debris from trees will stain the wood surface and the piles of decomposing organic matter will hold moisture, leading to mildew and rot. Use a heavy-duty broom to sweep your deck regularly, taking care to keep the gaps between boards clean. If leaves or twigs get stuck in the gaps, scrape them out with a putty knife. The more often you sweep, the easier it will be, especially if the leaves are dry.

To remove dirt and mildew and brighten the colour of your decking, once a year or so give it a more thorough cleaning. Use a specialist decking cleaner, such as Thompson's and follow the pack instructions. Using a long-handled stiff-bristled brush, scrub the deck with the solution. Rinse with buckets of clean water.
  If you have a covered or partially covered deck that is not built to withstand rain, clean it as you would an indoor hardwood floor – with a barely-damp mop or, on occasions, with a cleaner made especially for wood, such as Pledge Soapy Wood Cleaner. Do not soak the deck with water, or run the hose over it.

To remove stains and mildew, use a solution, made up from 40ml of oxygen bleach per 5 litres of warm water. Unlike chlorine bleach, which can break down the lignin that holds the wood together and

Fountains

Washing your fountain periodically with a solution of 1 part bleach to 10 parts water will inhibit algal growth.

To prevent mineral deposits from forming on bowls, the motor shaft, or other parts of the pump (which could cause it to fail), always use distilled water, rainwater or dehumidified water in the fountain. If your fountain is so big that using distilled water is not practical, treat the water with a mineral deposit inhibitor recommended by your local fountain or garden centre.

To remove mineral deposits – should they develop despite your best efforts – you will first need to know what your fountain bowl is made of.
• Some materials, such as resins and copper, are soft and should be cleaned with a cotton rag.
• Slate can be cleaned with a soft-bristled brush – but don't use soap. Slate can be porous; if it absorbs soap, your fountain could turn into a bubble bath.
• Other fountain bowl materials can be cleaned with an abrasive sponge and white vinegar or a mineral deposit cleaner, available at hardware stores and home improvement stores.

If your preventive maintenance is working, you may need to clean your fountain only once a year. If it is covered with mineral deposits, you will have to clean the parts more frequently – likewise if you are not using a water treatment product. In general, you should sterilise your fountain after you clean it and before you reassemble it by dipping all parts, including the pump, in the mild bleach solution mentioned above (1 part bleach to 10 parts water).

To clean the fountainhead, you will also need to know what it's made of:
• Most moulded fountainheads are cast from a polyester resin mixed with fillers such as powdered marble. These materials are strong but scratch easily, so the best way to clean them is with warm, soapy water and a soft sponge. Before using tile cleaners or other acids on a cast resin fountainhead, check it by putting a few drops of the cleaner on the bottom of the fountainhead and scrubbing it for a short while with a toothbrush.
• When cleaning concrete or natural stone, never use an acid cleaner. Washing-up liquid or bleach mixed with water, plus a scrubbing brush, will work fine.
• Clean slate in using the same method as for removing mineral deposits.

To clean a fountain pump, first check to see how well it's working. Most pumps have some sort of inlet strainers or screens to ensure that small pebbles and other debris don't get into the pump and jam or damage it. Watch the water flow in your fountain. If you notice it's slowing down, clean the pump before it clogs entirely, overheats and burns out. (Then you'll have to replace it.)

Garden furniture

Wooden chairs and tables should be sealed at the start of each season. Use teak oil or a wood stain, to do this. Metal furniture that has been poorly stored in the winter may develop rust spots. Use fine grade glasspaper to get these off, then apply a coat of clear varnish to protect.

Plastic resin furniture tends to need just a good clean. Avoid bleach-based spray

cleaners as they will pit the surface and – on greens particularly – you may suffer instant colour fade. Instead, make do with sudsy water from washing-up liquid. Use a large sponge or bundled rags to wipe down, then dry or leave out in the sun.

During the summer keep on top of the cleaning by keeping a pack of multi-surface wipes in the area where you store your tables and chairs. These are an effective and hygienic way to clean off the inevitable bird-droppings. You will minimise clean-ups by taking the extra minute each evening to tip chairs up against the table, so that the seats are protected from rain and dirt.

Garden ornaments

To clean or not to clean – that is the question when it comes to garden ornaments. Some people feel that a little algae, plus a bird dropping or two, give an ivy-clad concrete cherub a more natural look. But if you prefer to clean, here's how to do it.

Remember that much of what you will be cleaning is actually alive. Organic matter, such as algae, moss, mould and mildew, all make damp stone their host. Add to that dust and dirt, dead organic matter and bird droppings and you end up with quite a mess (or a lovely patina, if that's your view).

You can get rid of the organic matter and remove the rest with a simple, inexpensive solution of 100ml of bleach to 4 litres of water, with a squirt or two of washing-up liquid thrown in and worked into suds. Wear gloves to apply it with a long-handled brush and gently scrub until clean. Rinse with the garden hose. This works for most materials used for garden ornaments and statues, including concrete, stone and polyester resins.

Because bleach can damage plants – and the lawn – move the ornaments to the driveway or a path for cleaning. For anything too large to move, use the cleaning agent sparingly and rinse with a sponge and bucket of clean water instead of the hose. Don't ever use chlorine to clean a pond that contains fish.

If you clean a birdbath, be sure to flush out the cleaning solution completely.

To clean mirror balls, use a window-cleaning solution. Mix 100ml of white vinegar in 4 litres of warm water and add a squirt of washing-up liquid. Apply it with a spray bottle or a clean cloth. Gently scrub until clean and either rinse with a hose or dry with a dry towel or newspaper. If the ball is stainless steel, wax it with car wax once a year to renew its shine and give it a protective coating. And wipe out scratches with an car scratch remover.

Garden trellises

Trellises make attractive additions to a lawn or garden, but all those cracks and crevices provide a wealth of places for dirt and grime to hide.

To clean trellises with no plants attached, use a hose with a nozzle that sends the water out in a tightly focused stream. Use a stiff-bristled nylon or fibre brush to scrub dirty spots. If the trellises are wood, use the brush sparingly; you can use a freer hand on trellises made of plastic, glassfibre or metal. You could also use a power washer, available at tool-hire shops.

To attack mossy growth, mix a solution of 4 litres of water and 300ml of chlorine bleach in a bucket. Scrub the solution on with a brush. Rinse thoroughly using plain water.

Hoses

Hoses require little cleaning other than the removal of dirt by spraying water from the hose onto itself.

Always start cleaning garden hoses with the least abrasive method and work your way up. If you need extra cleaning power, dampen a rag in warm water and add to it some biodegradable soap (from camping stores). Rub it over the hose and use clean water to rinse. If there is still dirt stuck on the hose, use a vinyl cleaner on vinyl hoses or rubber hoses that are coated with vinyl. Follow the manufacturer's pack instructions.

If your hose is blocked up but there are no kinks in it, you may have a build-up of calcium deposits from minerals in the water. Bend the hose back and forth along the entire length to break up the build-up. If there's a nozzle on the business end of the hose, remove it and then turn on the water. This will help to flush out the loosened deposits.

Give your garden hose a long and happy life. To increase the life expectancy of your hose, here are some more things you can do to care for it:
• Although most hoses have UV retardants, it helps to remove your hose from strong sunlight and freezing temperatures. Over time, sunlight can cause the material to become brittle.
• While your hose is not in use, store it on a reel to prevent it from forming kinks or knots. Place the reel out of the sun or on the east side of the house (so it only gets the morning sun).
• For winter storage, drain the hose and store it indoors To drain it, first detach the hose from the tap. Starting at the end of the hose, pick it up so that the water runs through the hose ahead of you. Make large loops over your shoulder as you go. When you reach the end, all the water will have run out. If you have a hose that's too heavy to loop over your shoulder, make loops around a bench or on a raised patch of ground.
• At the end of the summer, place the hose out in the sun for two days to thoroughly dry it out.
• Store the hose flat in large relaxed loops. If you hang your hose, you will get kinks that may freeze and damage the material.
• Never walk on or drive over a hose. Hoses aren't designed to withstand that much external pressure.

Greenhouses

The cleaner a greenhouse, the healthier the plants housed there will be. Dust, debris and clutter are magnets for insects, diseases and harmful microorganisms. Dirty windows also block the sun, so can mean your plants will grow less well.

Dust plants to remove fungal spores (such as grey mould and powdery mildews) and mites. Most people hose off their plants, which is fine but tends to unsettle and spread the dust. An easier – and more effective – method is to vacuum them. Use an extension lead and your ordinary vacuum cleaner with a dusting attachment. This works best on sturdy leaves that you can hold in your hand while you quickly whisk the brush over the surface. Once a year is enough to halt the growth of the plant predators mentioned above.

Cut down on clutter in your greenhouse. Piles of dead plants, stacks of dirty pots and sacks spilling over with potting soil can all be places for insects and microorganisms to spend the winter. Remove all of these and any other clutter regularly. Either get rid of them or store them in a shed, garage or basement. Dead plant material is the worst offender. Purge dead plants and pick up dead leaves.

Keep your greenhouse weed-free to get rid of yet another source of food for insects and bacteria. Weeds also boost a greenhouse's humidity level, which will make conditions even riper for disease and pestilence. Keep a sack of hydrated lime on hand (but don't clutter up the greenhouse with it). Sprinkle it under benches and in corners to deter weed growth. It lasts for a long time and is non-toxic to humans. You can buy hydrated lime at your hardware store or the local feed and seed store.

Never use herbicides in your greenhouse. Wash the greenhouse windows at least once a year. Do it when you have the least amount of living plant material in your greenhouse – so before you bring in those new seeds or seedlings to get growing for spring transplanting. For most people, window-washing time is during the autumn. Your goal is to keep the glass or polyurethane as clear as possible, as well as to kill any harmful microbial growth on the inner surface. Use a mild washing-up liquid; it not only loosens dirt but also has ingredients that break up proteins and fats – and rupture the membranes of bacteria and fungi. Depending on the size of your greenhouse, either put the washing-up liquid in a hose end sprayer or mix it with water in a clean spray bottle. Rinse by spraying with the garden hose.

Gutters & downpipes

Water is your home's worst enemy and guttering and downpipes are an important line of defence. Keep them clean so that they can work properly.

Clean out gutters whenever they are blocked. Be on the look out for this in autumn, as leaves fall. Wear heavy gloves, as thorns and roof nails often end up in gutters and use a ladder tall enough to reach the gutters safely. Make sure someone else is holding the bottom of the ladder. Each time you move it to a new section, stop and check you have anchored the ladder securely and safely and that the rungs are square-on with the house before you begin your climb.

Make your own scoop using a large plastic milk carton. Cut the top off and you will have a handled container with a wide opening – just right for scooping out rubbish and easy to throw away afterwards. After you have removed all the debris, sluice it out with a hose.

Iron furniture

To clean a smooth piece of wrought iron, wipe first with a soft cotton rag, to remove dust and then wipe with furniture polish sprayed onto a clean section of the rag. If there's dirt stuck to the wrought iron, furniture polish may help lubricate and remove it.

To clean outdoor furniture that has a rusty finish or patina, let your item reach the desired rusty brown before you clean. Wipe off loose rust, dust or dirt with a rag. Then coat the piece with a clear lacquer paint (available at hardware stores) to protect it from the elements and to prevent any further rusting.

Outdoor furniture that isn't supposed to rust needs to be cleaned only when it looks dirty or has mud or grime caked on it. Remove dirt by spraying with a garden hose. Periodically check the piece for rust, which may start around areas such as bolts. If you see minor oxidation, gently use a dry wire brush to remove the rust. Wipe off any dust particles you create. Before applying touch-up paint to the surface, wipe the area clean with acetone or paint thinner on a cotton cloth. This will make the paint adhere better by removing oils that have transferred to the iron from your hands. It also will dissolve any remaining paint in the rusty area. Let the paint thinner dry before painting. Wear gloves and goggles, as acetone and paint thinner can be quite harsh to the skin and eyes. If your wrought iron is very rusty, you may have to take it to be sandblasted.

Outdoor toys

Cleaning at the start of spring isn't just about getting rid of rust. It's about safety too – because at the same time as you check the swing and climbing frame poles for wear and tear, you will also be able to tighten up any bolts that have become loose or moved out of the ground.

Cleaning the frames is a simple bucket of sudsy water and a sponge job. Most play equipment is made from aluminium or steel (if metal) or toughened plastic. Both respond well to basic cleaning.

Shift stubborn stains – bird droppings, mould from leaves that have pooled in crevices over the winter – using concentrated washing-up liquid on a pad. Dry off thoroughly, using old towels.

During the summer, keep a pack of multi-purpose wipes in the shed, so that you can regularly clean stains from the fabric tops of climbing frames and swing seats.

Patios

Patios end up stained by grease drippings from a barbecue, rusty metal furniture and decaying leaves. But because they are outside, you can use heavy-duty cleaners – and, if worst comes to worst, blast the dirt off with a power washer.

To reduce staining, sweep the leaves and other debris off your patio regularly. Use an outdoor-quality bristle broom or a rechargeable leaf blower.

Give your patio a more thorough cleaning, using a cleaner that is biodegradable and won't harm plants, such as Swarfega Patio and Drive Cleaner. Use a stiff-bristled brush (a long-handled one will be easier on your back and knees) to scrub. Rinse with a hose.

To deep-clean a stone, brick or concrete patio, use a pressure washer. Take care not to etch your patio material or injure yourself and never hold the jet too close to the patio surface. If you rent a power washer, be sure it comes with detailed safety instructions.

Cleaning for children

Children get into everything – and they put their hands and their playthings everywhere as well. When they are very small, it's important to keep baby bottles and feeding equipment as sterile as possible. Later, the tray on a toddler's highchair can be far dirtier than the floor – a worrying thought when you remember how they push food around on it. But getting into a simple but rigorous routine with everyday items and knowing how to clean their toys, bedding and equipment when necessary will protect your children from the germs and other nasties they are surrounded by.

Baby equipment

Babies require a lot of equipment and you will spend more time than you might imagine meticulously cleaning every item that your newborn baby comes into contact with.

Your baby's new immune system is just developing and needs to be carefully protected from 'everyday' germs that you'd shrug off without noticing. It's important to find the right balance between cleanliness and germ phobia. With a healthy baby, it isn't necessary to scrub down and sterilise everything in sight, but you should be careful with anything that may end up in your baby's mouth: bottles, teats, dummies and utensils used for feeding.

Sterilising baby bottles is a first year essential. Some bottles may be dishwasher safe but in reality you will only get a thorough clean by hand washing. You will need to rinse out again anyway, to ensure there are no traces of detergent. Wash the bottle and teat in hot water with sudsy washing-up water. Use a bottle brush and a teat brush to get right inside and so remove any caked-on milk in the interior corners. Force soapy water through the hole in the teat. Rinse thoroughly with clean water.

Now sterilise, according to the kind of steriliser you have. One that fits inside the microwave, holds up to eight bottles and takes only around five minutes, is easily the top choice. If you don't have a microwave, a bulkier, plug-in steam steriliser works just as well. Follow the instructions. Do not touch the teats when you go to make up the formula: use teat tongs instead, to manoeuvre them back onto the bottle.

To keep a changing table clean, use an antibacterial cleaning spray after each change. These don't need rinsing off. So give it a simple spray and wipe and you're done.

Antibacterial wipes are faster still: but at 2p–5p per go and up to 10 clean ups a day in those first, frantic weeks, using them can work out very expensive.

To clean prams and buggies sprinkle bicarbonate of soda on a damp paper towel or clean cloth and wipe down the item, then rinse with warm water. (Bicarbonate of soda is a mild alkali that can make dirt dissolve in water. It acts as a mild abrasive when not totally dissolved.) If that isn't strong enough, use the suds only from a solution of washing-up liquid to dab away at the dirt.

Cleaning highchairs The trick is to keep on top of the enormous amount of food that your toddler will push into every crevice of the chair. So after each meal, give a thorough wipe down. A blunt knife is useful for getting up dried in deposits. Use cleaning wipes and then follow with an

antibacterial cleaning spray. On the wooden surrounds use soapy water and then dry at once.

Cleaning a cot Use bicarbonate of soda (as described above) to wipe cot rails. Wash baby bed linen in a washing machine, using hot water, ideally at 60°C to kill bacteria.

Cleaning baby toys Remember that many plastic and rubber toys will stand up to the rigours of the dishwasher. Put them in regularly to keep microbes or organic material on the toys to a minimum. Wash stuffed animals in a washing machine, using hot water (60°C) to kill dust mites. If you feel this is too tough a treatment – many soft toys say surface wash with a sudsy cloth only – then use the freezer as a dust mite killer. Pop a toy into a sealed plastic bag for 48 hours: no creature can survive that.

Paddling pools

Since small children – and generally small children with muddy or grassy feet – are the main users, paddling pools tend to get dirty fast.

After each day's use, empty the pool and hose it out to prevent it from incubating germs. Store it under cover, upside down, or propped on its side, so that there is no risk of rainwater filling up inside – and creating a potential drowning hazard in your garden.

To remove scum from the sides, clean with a sponge or cloth dipped in a solution of 60ml bicarbonate of soda in 4 litres of warm water. Or wash with a solution of 1 tablespoon of washing-up liquid in 3 litres of water. Rinse with a hose.

Soft toys

Stuffed animals spend a lot of time on floors snuggling with loving children, who rub food and grime from their hands into the fake fur. Because of the variety of stuffing materials and accessories, such as clothing and ribbons, cleaning them can be trickier than simply throwing them in the washing machine.

Periodically dust stuffed animal toys using the vacuum cleaner brush attachment. Be sure not to suck up any loose buttons or clothing accessories. Preen fake hair with a clean hairbrush and then vacuum again to lift whatever the brush has loosened. (So that you won't get dirt and hair-product residue on the toys, buy a brush that you use only for this purpose.) To remove pet hair and lint, use a lint roller.

To remove light dirt, just lightly clean the surface. Wipe with a damp cloth, trying not to get moisture into the stuffing. Follow up by preening with a hairbrush.

To remove juice and other spills on stuffed animals, do what a live animal would do if you doused it with liquid: shake. Shake the toy, outside or in a bath, to keep the liquid from splashing onto anything else. This will remove some of the liquid without smearing it into the fur – or worse, the stuffing. Blot up as much remaining liquid as you can with kitchen roll. Never rub. Wet with a cloth or sponge. Blot again. Rinse the cloth or sponge. Repeat until the spill is gone.

For deeper cleaning, start by reading the care tag sewn into the seam. Machine-washing is safe for some stuffed animals, such as those filled with most synthetic fibres, but it can ruin others, such as those that have cardboard stiffeners. The same goes for drying: for some stuffed toys, a drier is fine, but other toys are stuffed so tightly that they will mildew or will never dry out.

If your toy isn't machine washable, surface-clean using a solution of warm water and mild washing-up liquid. Rub gently with a cloth or sponge dampened in

the solution, being sure not to soak the filling. Rinse by wiping with a cloth or sponge dampened with clear water. To maintain a consistent look to the surface, clean the whole animal and not just one spot. Air-dry and preen with a hairbrush.

If the tag says it's safe to wash, tie the stuffed toy up in a cloth bag, such as a laundry bag or pillowcase (but not a mesh bag), to protect the fur. It is safe to put several toy animals in the bag, as long as they fit loosely and aren't too big for the washing machine. Wash in cold water using a mild detergent on a gentle cycle. Don't use bleach or fabric softeners. Put the whole bag in the drier and tumble on the machine's gentlest setting.

Other toys

The main issue in cleaning toys is to never use anything toxic. Even if your son or daughter no longer chews on toys, hands will end up in mouths, since young children don't understand the concept of germs.

Wash toys regularly to keep them clean and bacteria-free. Wash rubber and plastic toys with warm water combined with a squirt of washing-up liquid. Wipe clean with a soft cloth or sponge. Be careful of painted-on features, such as faces, numbers or other designs. These could rub off. Dry with a cloth or leave to air-dry. For larger plastic toys, such as plastic sit-in cars and plastic playhouses, use a hose, a bucket of soapy water and a soft-bristled scrubbing brush.

Wipe down metal toys, such as tractors and cars, using a damp cloth. Water leads to rust, so avoid soap (since suds require rinsing) and don't submerge such toys. If a metal toy or a toy with metal parts gets wet, dry it quickly with a hair drier to avoid rusting. If there are batteries, beeping sounds or blinking lights, don't wet the toy. Water will completely ruin the circuitry.

Clean wooden toys with a mild solution of a neutral cleaner, such as Pledge Soapy Cleaner and water. (Follow the manufacturer's directions for amounts.) Use a cloth or soft-bristled brush. Don't soak or submerge the wooden toy. Instead, dip the cloth or brush in the soapy water and wipe the toy clean. Rinse with a clean cloth and plain water. Dry with a clean, dry towel. If the toy is scratched, splintered, or chipped, or if the water has raised the grain (making the wood feel rough), lightly sand it with fine glasspaper once the toy has dried.

If a wood toy has a natural, oil-based finish, reapply oil to keep the wood conditioned. Since toys often end up in children's mouths (wooden baby chew toys are expressly meant for this purpose), use a food-grade vegetable oil. Allow the oil to penetrate for about an hour and then wipe off the excess. It is especially important not to clean wooden toys with harsh chemicals, because wood absorbs such chemicals which could harm a child if ingested.

Clean Barbies and similar dolls by wiping with a cloth and water mixed with a little washing-up liquid. Wash hair with baby shampoo. (A drop of hair conditioner will soften the hair.) Don't use any heat source, such as a hair drier, to dry the hair, as that will turn it frizzy. Instead, comb the hair out gently, starting from the bottom and working up to remove tangles. Allow the doll to air-dry.

Cleaning for pets

Pets provide their owners with affection, companionship and entertainment. But whether you share your home with a Great Dane, a gerbil or a tank of tropical fish, there are a number of cleaning challenges that you have to contend with. Cats and dogs shed hair copiously, tread in mud and can leave their own distinctive odour. Fishtanks and small animal cages need regular cleaning to maintain the health of their inmates. Overleaf you will find solutions to most of the cleaning problems your pets present.

Animal bedding and cages

The fabric used for bedding for cats and small dogs is likely to be machine washable – so check the labels. Ideally, wash at 60°C to kill fleas and other insects and their eggs and then dry on a washing line.

Washing pet bedding in the bath is an option if it's too big for the machine (but remember to thoroughly clean the bath afterwards, with very hot water and bathroom cleaner). Or use either wicker or plastic – then place a cushion pad or quilt inside that can be easily washed. Or – our top cleaning and hygiene choice – use a cardboard box, that you can throw away every month. Wicker beds should be vacuumed each week. Every few months hose them down outside, on a sunny or blowy day, to ensure that the basket dries relatively quickly.

All cages need to be cleaned regularly Make life simple for yourself and have a second, spare cage for your bird or rodent to stay in. Knowing your pet is secure will mean you won't rush the cleaning. With gerbils, hamsters and other rodents, scoop out soiled wood shavings and replace with fresh daily. Each month, thoroughly disinfect the cage, using a specialist cleaner from the pet shop. Do not use kitchen spray cleaners on toys or bars as these can be too intense for your pet. Apply to the cloth and wipe each rung of the cage. Wipe again with a just damp cloth

Aquariums

Proper cleaning is a life-or-death issue for fish and should begin on the day you buy a new aquarium. Clean every piece of your new gear – tank, filters and accessories. Soap and detergent are not suitable as the residue they leave will hurt the fish. For new equipment, just use plain warm or cold water.

Check the aquarium's water once a week for its pH, nitrate, nitrite and ammonia levels, using water testing equipment sold at the pet shop. Check the chemical tolerances of your particular fish species, so you will know when it's time to change the water. How many fish you have, how big they are, the species, the size of the tank, your lighting and the kind of filtration you are using, all affect how often you must change the water. You should never change all the water at once. Just change 10 to 25 per cent of the water in your aquarium and expect to do it about every two weeks.

To change the water round up enough buckets to handle 10 to 25 per cent of the water in your tank. Use a siphon hose to draw the water out. A clear hose is best, so you can see what you are sucking up.

Don't refill the aquarium with water straight from the tap. Nearly all tap water has chlorine added and that will hurt your fish. Many pet shops will test a sample for you or you can use a home water chemical test kit. To remove the chlorine, either use a dechlorinating product, or let the water sit in a fresh bucket for 24 hours before pouring it in to the tank – this will have given the chlorine time to dissipate naturally. In any case, make sure the new water is about the same temperature – within one or two degrees – as the water left in the aquarium.

To remove algae use algae scrubbing pads (available at at aquarium shop or pet shop) and clean the inside walls of your aquarium whenever the fuzzy green stuff becomes visible. If you don't like sloshing around in the water with your hands, try a magnetic cleaning system. One magnet, attached to a scrubbing pad, goes on the inside of the glass and another magnet goes on the outside for dragging the scrubbing pad around. Remember, algae thrive on light, so the more light your aquarium gets the more algae you will have to clean up.

Clean the filter in your tank once a week – or more often, depending on the feeding habits of your fish and how many fish you have. Most tanks have a mechanical filter and models vary; follow the instructions that come with yours for removing, cleaning and replacing the filter. A clean filter means better water, which means healthier fish.

Another filtering tool is carbon. It gives your water a sparkling-clear look by removing the yellowish cast caused by food and waste. Carbon may already be a part of your mechanical filter. If not, you can buy a carbon holder or even make your own. Put the carbon (available at the aquarium store or pet shop) into an old pair of tights, tie a tight knot to secure and cut away excess fabric. Place the carbon filter where it will get good water flow in the tank.

To thoroughly clean an old tank – especially if fish have died in the tank – remove any fish to another water-filled container and empty everything out. Refill, with fresh water and add 2 teaspoons of bleach for every 4 litres of water. Let it sit for at least 30 minutes. Empty the tank, rinse it well and then refill. Now neutralise any bleach residue by adding a chlorine neutraliser (available from pet shops). Empty the water once again and rinse. Then fill your aquarium with the water that you have let sit for a day and put the fish back in.

Because tank cleaning is such a chore here are ways to cut down how often it needs to be done:
• **Keep it out of direct sunlight** and you'll grow less algae. You will also have the same problem if you leave your aquarium lights on for too long.
• **Start with freshwater fish.** They are

AN UNDERWATER DIRT DEVIL

The gravel at the bottom of your aquarium isn't just decorative. It's also a biological filter that traps gunk in the water. Give it a gentle vacuuming each time you change your aquarium's water with a vacuum you can make yourself.

1 Attach a clear plastic siphon hose to the top of a small plastic soft drink bottle. (The hose needs to be large enough to fit tightly over the bottle and to run out into a bucket at the other end.) Cut the bottom off the bottle. Then place the bottle on the bottom of the tank. When the siphon starts drawing water, it will suck up the dirt, waste and old food without disturbing the gravel.

2 Move from one patch of gravel to the next, working your way across the aquarium floor.

3 Since you will be using this technique at water-changing time, you will have to stop when you have removed your target amount of water. It may take you two sessions to cover the entire aquarium floor.

4 You can also install a special filter under the gravel, which will reduce the need for vacuuming.

less sensitive to variations in the chemical levels in the water so even if you get it slightly wrong, they should still be safe. Tracking the salt levels of a saltwater tank is yet another thing to do that could push a beginner over the edge.
• **Don't give your fish too much food.** Fish don't have fridges, so the leftovers float around, driving up the levels of harmful chemicals. Watch your fish at feeding time. When they begin to slow down their rate of eating, dinner's over so don't add more food.
• **Inspect your fish every day** to see whether they have any injuries, infections or parasites. When you buy new fish, let them stay in a 'guest room' for a month – a separate quarantine tank – so you can monitor them for diseases that could kill the rest of your fish.

Birdbaths, bird feeders & birdhouses

Keep birdbaths, feeders and birdhouses free of fungi, algae and bacteria and the birds will keep using them happily for years. All you need to maintain them is an old scrubbing brush and a tired toothbrush.

Clean a birdbath once a week during warm weather. Birdbaths with stale standing water can turn into fertile breeding grounds for mosquito larvae and other insects, so dumping out old water and cleaning inside is essential.

First, use a scrubbing brush with stiff bristles and warm water to scrub out the birdbath. If the bath has a telltale ring from algae or other deposits or feels slimy to the touch, mix a solution of 1 part bleach to 10 parts water in a clean bucket and use that to scrub the bath. Wear rubber gloves to protect your hands. If you don't like the notion of using bleach, mix equal parts of white vinegar and water and scrub. Rinse with fresh water and air-dry.

Clean bird feeders every two weeks all through the year. This is because birdseed and other bird food gets damp and mouldy in humid conditions and the birds feeding at your trough may get sick. If you can, take your wooden feeder apart. Dust off the pieces with a wire brush and then scrub with warm water and a stiff-bristled scrubbing brush. If the feeder is really dirty, wear rubber gloves and mix 1 part bleach to 10 parts water in a clean bucket. Vigorously scrub it, both inside and out. Rinse thoroughly and then dry. For plastic or metal feeders, brush them out, then rinse with warm water and dry with a soft cloth, or simply leave to air-dry.

Clean a birdhouse during cold weather when birds aren't feathering their nests inside. If the birdhouse has a removable side or top panel, take it off and dip the pieces into a solution of 1 part bleach to 10 parts water. With an old toothbrush, dig into the cracks and crevices – this is where feather mites, which feed on bird feathers, often lurk. You don't want these bugs infesting the next generation to take up residence in your birdhouse. To guard against mites, as well as fleas, flies, larvae and lice use an aviary dusting powder, which is available from pet shops.

Fishponds

Even a small pond is a complex ecological system and you need the right mix of two plant groups – submerged plants to oxygenate the water and floating plants to provide shade – to help control algae. The mix must be in the right proportions to work effectively.

Routine pond maintenance consists mostly of removing debris such as dead leaves from the water. Use a long-handled swimming pool skimmer net. Don't expect your pond to be crystal clear. The water should be a pale green. Environmental balance takes a long time to establish, so don't be too quick to upset it by emptying and refilling the pond.

4 Start removing the remaining water with a pump or siphon. As the water level drops, remove the submerged plants and put them in the paddling pool, too.

5 While there is still water at the bottom of the pond, clean the sides with a soft-bristled scrubbing brush. Continue to drain until the bottom layer of dirt is in sight. Then stop pumping and remove the bottom debris with a dustpan.

6 Rinse the sides of the pool with a hose and then remove the pump and rinse. Gently scrub the bottom.

7 Replace the plants before you begin refilling. Use a water conditioner, available at pet or aquarium stores, to neutralise chlorine in the new water. Return the water that you have saved in the paddling pool and other containers to the pond and let the pond warm up slightly before returning the fish.

A major pond cleaning is called for when there is a lot of muck or too many fish in the water. The pond may have been overstocked, or the fish may have multiplied. In either case, you may have to find new homes for some of your scaly friends. A rule of thumb is that each fish in a pond should have about a barrel of water. The best time – and many experts say the only time – to clean a pond is in early spring, when cool temperatures provide a less stressful environment for the fish and plants. Even so, always keep the fish and plants that you remove from the pond in the shade to avoid stressing them.

Here's what to do:

1 Begin by removing the edge plants and then the floating ones, pot and all. Put them in the shade.

2 Use a bucket to draw water off the top (the cleanest part) of the pond. Place a children's paddling pool in a shady spot and fill it with the water, which will be the right pH and temperature to hold the fish. Save as much of the rest of the pond water as you can in extra containers, unless it is really disgusting.

3 When the pond has been half drained, remove the fish with a net and transfer them to the paddling pool. Cover it with a mesh screen, to stop any aspiring flying fish and deter predatory cats and other animals.

Kennels

If your pet has a kennel outside, you don't have to change the bedding as often as you change your own sheets. But at least once a month is not too often to keep fleas and mites and other kinds of insect pests at bay and make it a clean and comfortable haven for your dog to sleep in.

Start cleaning a kennel by treating it like you would a teenager's bedroom. Get everything out. If you use straw, throw it away. If your dog likes to curl up in blankets, put them in the washing machine. Hose down the kennel, inside and out. You might need to lift one end to drain all the water. Then get ready to scrub.

When washing a kennel, don't use anything that you wouldn't want your pet to lick up or ingest. Chemical household cleaners will make a home sparkle. But dogs aren't as particular about the way their home looks as they are about the way it smells. A pine-scented habitat might smell deliciously clean to you, but your dog might disagree. Instead, use a plastic-bristled brush to apply an organic cleaner or use a homemade solution of

4 tablespoons of lemon extract or lemon juice with 4 litres of water. Or mix 100ml of vinegar to 300ml of water.

Replacing the bedding is the last step If your dog likes to lie on straw, put in some fresh straw and sprinkle it with bicarbonate of soda to make the freshness last longer. If your pet prefers blankets, let the washed blankets dry in the sun for extra freshness; then sprinkle them with a little bicarbonate of soda.

Litter trays

How, and how often, you clean your cat's litter tray depends on the kind of litter you use and the type of tray – and how fussy your cat is. With most cats, the cleaner the better.

Here are the basics:
- **To clean a litter tray,** remove solids daily – and don't forget, or your fastidious cat may find another spot.
- **With clumping litter,** remove the faeces and urine clumps with a slotted scoop available at pet and discount stores. Clumping litter should be dumped and the tray washed about every week – sooner if your nose or eyes say it is time.
- **For non-clumping litter,** remove the solids daily with a scoop and change the litter and wash the tray at least twice a week or more often if needed.

DON'T USE PERFUMED LITTER

You had the best intentions in the world sprinkling a deodorising powder on the litter tray. But cats' noses are extremely sensitive – and unpredictable. Some cats take offence at even such a mild, inoffensive substance as bicarbonate of soda.

If your cat suddenly stops using its litter tray and has substituted something else – such as the dining room rug – scent may be the problem. Switch to a different litter and see if that helps. If not, buy a new box. A lingering, if faint, urine smell embedded in the plastic could also be why your cat is going to the toilet elsewhere.

- **To clean self-cleaning litter trays,** which can include motors and other moving parts, follow the manufacturer's directions carefully.

To wash the tray, use a little washing-up liquid and water and scrub with a stiff brush. Avoid using any cleaner with a strong smell, such as scented detergents or ammonia, which could turn up a sensitive feline nose. But do disinfect with a solution of 1 part chlorine bleach to 10 parts water. Rinse thoroughly with plain water – your cat may stop using the tray if it smells of washing-up liquid – and if possible dry in the sunshine – it's a natural disinfectant. Or wipe dry with a clean cloth or paper towels before adding fresh litter.

To stop footprints emanating from the tray area, put a piece of carpet or a rubber mat at the spot where your cat leaves the tray.

Pet equipment

Keep your pet's things clean: their bedding and bowls, toys and sweaters (if they wear them). Cleaning will prolong the life of the equipment, keep your pet healthy and reduce pet odours.

Wash food and water bowls daily to avoid the growth of bacteria. Put them in the dishwasher, if they are dishwasher safe. You can include them with your own dishes – the high dishwasher temperatures will disinfect everything. Or hand-wash using hot, soapy water. (Do this separately from your dishes.) Keep two sets of dishes for your pet and rotate them. Stainless steel bowls are usually easiest to clean.

Clean leads periodically to remove dirt and salt, which can corrode the metal parts. Soak non-leather leads in a sink full of warm water with a squirt of washing-up liquid and a dash of liquid fabric softener (to keep the lead soft, not stiff). Rub clean with a sponge. Rinse in a sink full of clean, warm water. Don't wash leashes in the washing machine, because they could get tangled and the metal clasps could dent your machine. Hang up to dry.

Hand-wash dog coats using the same care you would use on your own clothes – unless the care instructions say otherwise. Most are made from the same materials as human sweaters – wool or acrylic. Fill a basin with lukewarm water and add a gentle fabric wash, such as Woolite, or a squirt of mild washing-up liquid. Soak and then gently rub out any stains. Rinse thoroughly in clear, lukewarm water. Gently wring the sweater out. Wrap it in a clean towel to remove moisture. Lay the towel out on a flat surface and work the sweater into shape with your hands. Let it dry.

Wash pet toys regularly to keep them clean and bacteria free. Wash rubber and plastic toys in a sink full of hot, soapy water with a dash of bleach. Scrub with a nylon-bristled brush. Stuffed toys and rope toys can go in the washing machine and tumble dryer. When they fray, or the stuffing starts to escape, throw them away and get your pet a new toy.

To wipe unsavoury dribbles off the Frisbee (or rubber ball) you've been throwing for your dog, use a wet wipe. Take along a portable travel carton of wipes when you play fetch in the park – or any other time you are away from a garden hose or tap.

Cleaning up after your pet

Furry pets and a pristine house are not an easy combination. They spread hair on carpets and furniture, walk muddy paws on clean floors, are messy eaters. And then there are the accidents, which need swift attention if they are not to stain and leave a lasting odour.

Removing pet hair from furniture Start with the vacuum cleaner. Buy a lint-brush attachment for your vacuum if you don't already have one. This gadget first prises up

and then sucks up short, wiry hairs that have imbedded themselves in your upholstery. As an alternative, wear a damp rubber glove and rub your hand across the sofa cushion. The hair will clump together for easy removal.

Stopping your pet from shedding Use the brush attachment on your vacuum to literally hoover your pet. As long as you are careful and your pet does not mind the sucking action and noise, this is a good way to make a pre-emptive strike against hair that is bound to fall out. You might find that your dog, or even your cat, loves the attention. It feels like a pet massage. If your pet is afraid of the vacuum, regular combing or brushing will do.

Cleaning up pet vomit Start with the chunks of solid stuff. Remove them with a paper towel or spatula. If the vomit is on a hard surface, such as a vinyl or wood floor, simply wipe up the liquid with moist paper towels and then thoroughly mop the spot with clean water.

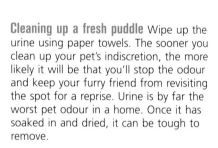

Cleaning pet vomit from fabric, carpet or rugs If your pet has thrown up on a carpet or upholstered furniture, blot up as much of the liquid as possible using paper towels. Next, apply a cleaner with active enzymes, designed especially for pet mess. Available at pet stores, these cleaners actually digest the proteins found in the vomit. They usually take a while. So let the cleaner stand for as long as the product's directions suggest. Then, for clothing, wash and rinse or dry-clean according to label instructions. For carpeting or furniture, blot with clean, cool water to rinse (but avoid using too much water, especially if there is a pad under the carpet or stuffing in the upholstered furniture). Remove excess liquids by either repeatedly blotting with fresh, dry paper towels or using a wet vac. As with any pet accident, the key to success is to clean the mess up immediately.

Cleaning up pet faeces Begin by removing any solids with tissue paper. Flush down the toilet. If there is little or no residue (as with firm faeces on a hard floor), clean with soapy water and paper towels. Then rinse with clean water and paper towels. If there is residue (as with loose faeces on a carpet), follow the steps listed for cleaning up vomit: blot up as much of the liquid as possible using paper towels and apply a specialist pet cleaner. Wash and rinse according to the type of material.

Cleaning up a fresh puddle Wipe up the urine using paper towels. The sooner you clean up your pet's indiscretion, the more likely it will be that you'll stop the odour and keep your furry friend from revisiting the spot for a reprise. Urine is by far the worst pet odour in a home. Once it has soaked in and dried, it can be tough to remove.

Removing urine from a carpet Soak up as much of the liquid as possible with paper towels. Then cover the spot with a thick layer of dry paper towels, with newspaper on top of that. (Make sure the newsprint doesn't rub off on the carpet.) Stand on the padding for a minute or so. Then remove the soaked padding and take it to your pet's bathroom area – the cat's litter box or the dog's designated outdoor area – to lure your pet there the next time. Repeat the process. Apply a specialist pet cleaner, designed to digest proteins, to help remove the urine smell.

Then rinse the accident zone by blotting with a cloth soaked in clean water. Remove excess water by blotting with paper towels (as above). Don't use fragrant chemical cleaners, vinegar or ammonia. As with the urine smell, these odours could draw the pet back to the scene of the crime.

Stain buster guide

Almost any surface can become permanently stained if you don't
know how to deal with the substances that you have dropped
on it. From hard surfaces like porous marble worktops and
concrete, to soft carpets and textiles, most will respond if dealt
with swiftly and correctly. Protein stains such as egg, blood,
grease and pet accidents are frequent offenders and can stain for
good if left. Here's how to blitz just about anything that you drop
unsuspectingly in your home.

Dealing with stains

No matter how careful and houseproud you are, accidents do happen. This chapter looks at how to deal with everyday spills and soiling, including how to identify the kind of stain and the steps you can take to deal with it, from the lightest options to the most drastic and heavyweight solutions.

Take immediate action

Taking swift action can often stop a spill or sudden accident from turning into a stain. That doesn't mean that you should panic. Things usually get more difficult when the spill has dried up, and become 'locked' into the fibres of the material that it landed on. Even on a hot day, most things will not dry out immediately.

Stains aren't really very mysterious. Most fall into one of four main categories: protein, oil-based, tannin and dye. The rest are usually a combination of those categories. By understanding what is in a stain, you can determine the best and safest way to remove it.

Before moving on to stain-removal specifics, read the general guidelines below. Always consider the material on which the spill has occurred. Some treatments may remove the stain, but if the fabric is delicate, it may be ruined in the process. So you must always make a judgment about whether the stained item can be safely treated, or if the lesser of two evils is actually to live with the stain but keep a favourite item in one piece.

There are three main categories of textiles that can be stained: washable fabrics (clothing, linens and towels), carpets and upholstered furniture. Below are general steps to follow when trying to remove stains from all three.

Washable fabrics One of the main advantages with washable items is that you have access to both sides of the stain. That simply isn't possible with a fitted carpet or fixed upholstery on sofas. Pre-treatment often consists of pushing the stain out from the back side of the fabric. Attempt stain treatment on washable fabrics using the steps below.

1 Remove as much of the stain-causing material as possible by blotting with paper towels or scraping with a dull knife.

2 Pre-treat the stain by soaking or applying a cleaning solution. It helps to lightly agitate the fabric being soaked or to gently rub together the stained fabric with your hands.

3 Launder in your washing machine according to the instructions on the fabric's care label.

4 If necessary, repeat the preceding steps, possibly using a stronger cleaning solution.

Carpeting Typically you have access to the top side only for stain removal. But you should never soak carpet stains, because most carpets and rugs have rubber or synthetic-based lining under them. Getting cleaning solutions into those pads can actually attract dirt and lead to other problems, such as mildew and glue deterioration. Try these methods instead.

1 Remove as much of the stain-causing material as you can by blotting with paper towels or scraping with a dull knife. When blotting up a large stain, always blot from the edge of the stain to the centre to contain it. Standing on the blotting paper will increase its ability to blot up more. Jump up and down if you like.

2 Avoid rubbing, which can push the stain deeper into the pile. Avoid using a circular motion, which can destroy a carpet's texture.

3 Because you should never soak a carpet, spray bottles are good for applying a small amount of water-based cleaning solution and rinse water. You can buy them very cheaply from garden centres.

4 To dry patches of carpet that have been rinsed with water, lay a pad of paper towels on the spot and place a weight, such as a brick, on the pad. To prevent transferring colour from the brick to the carpet, put the brick in a plastic bag or wrap it in foil. When the carpet is dry, remove the paper towels. Brush the carpet pile to restore a consistent texture.

Upholstery You rarely have a chance to get at both sides of the stain with upholstered furniture. Even if you can remove the covering material, most manufacturers warn against washing cushion covers separately from the cushions because of possible shrinkage and fading. So one small mark can quickly escalate to a big washing job. The trick, as with carpeting, is to remove the stain from the top side without soaking the cushion beneath. So follow the steps for removing carpet stains, listed above, to deal with similar upholstery stains.

Protein-based stains

Baby food and formula milk, cream or cheese-based foods, eggs, faeces and urine are all protein stains.

Fresh protein stains Cold water may be all you will need to remove them. Don't use hot water, because it can 'cook' the proteins, causing the stain to coagulate between the fibres in the fabric and become locked there for ever. For washable fabrics, soak in cold water for half an hour, put the stain under running cold water and gently rub the fabric against itself to loosen the stain. Launder in the washing machine in warm water.

Old or dried-on protein stains With this kind of stain, you may have to take your stain-removal tactics to the next level. Soak washable fabrics for half an hour in a solution of 1 teaspoon of liquid detergent (choose a biological one containing enzymes – the label will say whether it has them) per 2 litres of cold water. Follow this soaking by laundering the fabric in your washing machine in warm water. Inspect the item before drying. If the stain is still there, soak the fabric for an additional half hour and then wash again. If the stain remains after that, your only option may be to add the recommended amount of oxygen bleach to the next wash cycle, especially if the stain was caused by a coloured ice cream or baby food.

Fresh protein stain in carpeting or upholstery Spray with cold water and blot, repeating until the stained area comes clean.

Dried protein stain in carpeting or upholstery Lightly apply a solution of ¼ teaspoon mild washing-up liquid (one that doesn't contain lanolin) in 1 litre cold water. Apply the solution to a cloth and use a blotting motion to work the solution into the affected area.

Blot with a clean paper towel to remove the solution. Rinse by lightly spraying the stain with water and then blotting. Do this until all the suds are gone. Then spray again lightly with water. Don't blot. Instead, lay a pad of paper towels over the spot, put a weight on it, and let it dry.

If the stain persists, repeat the procedure with a stronger solution: ½ teaspoon of liquid detergent (a biological one containing enzymes) per litre of cold water.

If that still doesn't completely remove the stain, moisten the stained tufts with a solution of 3 per cent hydrogen peroxide – you can buy this from the chemist where it is sold as a mouthwash. Let it stand for an hour. Blot and repeat until the carpet or upholstery is stain free. No rinsing is necessary following this procedure, because light will cause the peroxide to change to water. To dry, use the method mentioned above involving a pad of paper towels and a weight. But be careful: hydrogen peroxide is bleach and can drastically fade colours.

Oil-based stains

Oil-based stains aren't as difficult to get rid of as most people think. They include auto grease or motor oil, hair oil and mousse, hand lotion, kitchen grease, lard, butter, bacon, oils, ointments, salad dressing and suntan lotion. Many pre-wash stain-removal products, such as Vanish and Shout, are formulated with special solvents for removing oil and grease.

Oil-based stains in washable fabrics Pre-treat new and old stains with a commercial pre-wash stain remover. Alternatively, apply liquid detergent, or a paste made from powder detergent mixed with water, directly to the stain. Work the detergent into the stain. Immediately after pre-treatment, launder the item in the washing machine in hot water (if that is safe for the fabric). Before drying the fabric, inspect it. If the stain is still evident, repeat the process until it is gone. For heavy stains, lay the stain face down on a clean white towel or stack of paper towels and press a dry-cleaning solvent – sold in supermarkets as dry clean stain remover – onto the stain, forcing it out and into the towels. Repeat and launder.

Oil-based stains in carpets and upholstery Apply methylated spirits to a clean white cloth or white paper towel and blot the stain. Discard the dirty towels and repeat using fresh paper towels and alcohol until the stain is gone. Don't let the alcohol penetrate the carpet backing, as it can destroy the rubber lining. If that doesn't remove the stain, try the method recommended on page 117 for removing dried protein stains from carpeting or upholstery.

Tannin stains

Alcoholic drinks, coffee or tea without milk, fruits and fruit juices, soft drinks and wine all have tannin as the base of their stains. Most jams also contain tannins, but cherry and blueberry jellies should be treated as dye stains.

Tannin stains in washable fabric Soak for half an hour in a solution of 1 teaspoon liquid detergent (choose a biological one containing enzymes) per 2 litres of warm water. Then launder in the washing machine in the hottest water that is safe for the fabric, using laundry detergent. Don't be tempted to give it a quick go with soap first: natural soaps – including soap flakes, bar soap, and hand wash detergent containing soap – make tannin stains harder to remove. To remove stubborn tannin stains, you may need to wash with bleach. If all the sugars from one of these stains aren't removed, they may turn brown when put into the dryer, as the sugar will caramelise. So check first before you attempt to dry.

Tannin stains in carpeting or upholstery Lightly apply a solution of ¼ teaspoon mild dishwashing liquid and 1 litre water. Use a blotting motion to work the solution into the affected area. Blot with a clean paper towel to remove the solution. Rinse by lightly spraying with water and blotting to remove excess water. Do this until all the suds are gone. Then spray lightly with water again, but don't blot. Instead, lay a pad of paper towels down, weight it, and let it dry. If the blemish persists, repeat the procedure using a solution of ½ teaspoon liquid detergent (a biological one containing enzymes) per litre of water. If that doesn't completely remove the stain, moisten the tufts in the stained area with 3 per cent hydrogen peroxide.

Let stand for one hour. Blot and repeat until the stain has disappeared. No rinsing is necessary following this procedure. To dry, lay down the weighted pad of paper towels mentioned above.

Dye stains

Blackcurrant, cherry, grass and mustard are all dye-based stains and can be real nightmares to shift. But all is not lost.

Dye stains in washable fabrics Pre-treat with a commercial pre-wash stain remover. Or apply liquid laundry detergent directly to the stain, work the detergent into the stain, and rinse well. Next, soak the fabric in a diluted solution of oxygen bleach (identified as 'all-fabric' on the label), following the directions on the packaging. Launder. Check to see whether the stain is still there. If so, try soaking the garment in a solution of chlorine bleach and water, following dilution instructions on the label but be aware that you may be putting your item at risk.

Dye stains in carpet or upholstery You may have to call a professional cleaner or, in the case of a solid-coloured carpet, cut the stained part out and patch it with clean carpet. But before you go that far, try the procedure described on page 118 for tannin stains on carpet or upholstery. It helps to go very carefully: when you are using hydrogen peroxide, dab a little onto a cotton bud and try to absorb the stain from the carpet into the bud.

Combination stains

Many common stains are a mixture of both oils or waxes and dyes – stains from makeup are always a type of combination stain. They are commonly divided into two categories for the purposes of treatment.

Group A combination stains include those from lipstick, eye makeup including mascara, pencil, liner and most kinds of eye shadows, various types of furniture polish and, perhaps worst of all, shoe polish.

Group B combination stains include chocolate, gravy, hair spray, face makeup (foundation, powder, blusher), peanut butter and tomato-based foods.

To remove these stains, you must first remove the oily or waxy portion, and then you can try to remove the dye. As with any tough stain, your success is not guaranteed. But, by following the steps below, you do stand a chance, especially if you get to the stain while it's fresh.

Washable fabrics with stains in Group A Start by applying a dry-cleaning stain remover. Next, rub with a liquid detergent and scrub in hot water to remove the oily or waxy part. Then launder, using a laundry detergent and an oxygen or all-fabric bleach. Inspect before drying. If the stain persists, wash with chlorine bleach.

Washable fabrics with stains in Group B Skip the dry-cleaning solvent. Rub the stain with a liquid laundry detergent and launder in the washing machine in the hottest water possible for the fabric. If that doesn't work, try oxygen bleach and then, if that fails, chlorine bleach (but only on white fabrics).

Combination stains in carpets and upholstery Begin by removing the oily or waxy part first. Apply methylated spirits to a clean white cloth or white paper towel and blot the stain. Discard the dirty towels and repeat using fresh paper towels and

more methylated spirits until the stain is gone. Don't let the alcohol penetrate the carpet backing, as it could destroy the rubber lining.

If the alcohol treatment doesn't remove the stain, lightly apply a solution of ¼ teaspoon of mild washing-up liquid (one that doesn't contain lanolin) and 1 litre of water. Use a blotting motion to work the solution into the affected area. Blot with a clean paper towel to remove the solution. Rinse by lightly spraying with water and blotting. Do this until all the suds are gone. Then spray again lightly with water. Instead of blotting this time, lay a pad of paper towels down, put a weight on it, and let it dry.

Finally, if that doesn't completely remove the stain, moisten the stained tufts with 3 per cent hydrogen peroxide and let stand for one hour. Blot and repeat until the stain is gone. No rinsing is necessary following this procedure. To dry, use a pad of paper towels and weight.

Other stains

Stains produced by perspiration, glue, paint, mud and nail polish are all fairly hard to remove and need to be dealt with differently from the previous categories.

Deodorant and perspiration stains Treat these as you would dye stains. The aluminium or zinc salt build-up from deodorants can make them particularly stubborn.

Removing glue Begin by scraping off whatever you can with a dull knife (rubbing ice on the glue first to harden it). If the glue is white school glue, treat it as you would a protein-based stain, so don't use hot water – the hot water could cook the proteins. If it is model-aeroplane glue, treat it as an oil-based stain. If the glue won't come out, place the stain face-down on absorbent paper towels. To force the stain out, blot the back of the fabric with a cloth moistened with dry-cleaning solvent.

Removing emulsion paint Treat while it is wet – immediately is best. Soak the fabric in cold water and then wash it in cold water with laundry detergent. If the paint has dried, even for as little as six hours, treat it as you would one of the Group A combination stains (page 119).

Removing gloss paint Spot treat while it is still wet using paint thinner or white spirit and a sponge or cloth until the paint is loosened and as much is removed as possible. Before it dries, wash in hot water and detergent.

Removing mud Handle mud as you would a protein-based stain, with one exception: it's best to wait until mud has dried before cleaning it. Once it has dried, scrape off the excess solids. Then follow the protein-stain procedures.

Removing rust stains If a rust stain remains after removing the mud, treat it with a commercial fabric stain rust remover. Since rust removers can be toxic, follow the directions on the container carefully. A solution of lemon juice and salt sometimes removes rust. Sprinkle salt on the stain, squeeze lemon juice on it, and put the item in the sun to dry. Be sure to test the lemon juice first, since it can bleach some fabrics. Don't use chlorine bleach: it will make rust stains permanent.

Removing nail polish Blot with a clean cloth moistened with acetone or nail polish remover until the stain is gone. If possible, lay the stain face down on white paper towels and blot from the back side to force the stain out the way it came in.

Removing yellowing from white fabrics Fabrics can take on a yellowish tinge for several reasons: not enough detergent in a wash cycle, too much detergent, insufficiently hot wash temperatures, colour transfer from other items while washing, or the loss of a fabric's artificial whiteners. Your best bet for restoring brightness and whiteness is to launder with the correct amount of detergent – read the labels to find one that has both bleach and optical brighteners in it. Most biological powders have the greatest whitening power. If that doesn't work, try oxygen bleach. As a final resort, try a cycle with chlorine bleach.

Cleaning emergencies

Chewing gum on the sofa, a flea infestation, baby sick or an unfortunate accident by a kitten or puppy, a biro that has leaked sticky ink in your pocket or handbag, coffee or wine pooling on a light-coloured carpet, nail polish on a fine wooden floor or candle wax on polished furniture – life is just full of unwelcome surprises. Here's a fast-find guide to the most likely of household disasters. If something messy has just happened, don't despair – chances are we've got advice on the fastest and most effective ways to deal with it right here.

Animal accidents on carpets

Your main aim is to remove any solid matter and liquid before it soaks right through the carpet or anyone treads in it. To speed things up, if you have a pet that frequently messes, keep a crisis kit in the understairs cupboard (or somewhere that you can reach fast). Include: paper towels, plastic grocery bags (for disposing of solids and used paper towels) and an enzyme-based cleaner (available at pet shops). Start by removing any solids. Then blot up as much of the liquid content as possible, using paper towels. You will soak up maximum liquid if you stand on the paper towels (in shoes) or press a weight onto them. Soak the accident site in the enzyme cleaner. Let sit for a few minutes and then blot up. Rinse the residue with water to avoid leaving smells that might draw the pet back to use the same spot.

Baby sick or nappy contents on clothes or upholstery

First try cold water, which may be all you will need if these protein stains are fresh. Don't use hot water, since it can 'cook' the proteins, causing the stain to coagulate between the fibres in the fabric. Soak washables in cold water for half an hour, run the stain under cold tap water and gently rub the fabric against itself to loosen the stain. Then launder in your washing machine in warm water. For carpeting or upholstery, spray with cold water and blot with a clean cloth or paper towels. Repeat until the stain is gone. If residue remains, soak the accident site in enzyme cleaner. Wash and rinse according to product directions.

Blood on fabric or carpet

If it's fresh, cold water should be all you will need to remove this protein stain. Don't use hot water, since hot water can cook the proteins, causing the stain to coagulate between the fibres in the fabric. Soak washables in cold water for half an hour, then run the stain under the cold tap and gently rub the fabric against itself to loosen the stain. Wash in warm water. For carpeting or upholstery, spray with cold water and blot with a clean white towel repeating until clean.

Candle wax on fabric or carpet

If the wax is still soft, blot up the excess with paper towels. If it is hard, gently scrape the excess with a dull knife. Next, lay a plain brown bag or white paper towel (no dyes or printing inks) over the wax and run a hot iron over the paper. The heat will melt the wax and the paper will absorb it. Continue by moving the bag or paper towel around to unsaturated sections until all the wax is absorbed. Remove residue by blotting with a dry-cleaning solvent such as Spotless Dry Clean Liquid. Be sure to test the solvent first on an inconspicuous spot.

Chewing gum on upholstery, or carpet

Use an ice cube to remove chewing gum from a variety of places – clothing, upholstery, carpeting and hard surfaces. Simply rub the ice on the gum until it freezes and hardens. To avoid water drips, put the ice in a plastic bag before rubbing it on the gum. Scrape away the hardened gum with a dull knife. If residue remains, remove it by blotting with a dry-cleaning solvent, such as Spotless Dry Clean Liquid. Be sure to test the solvent first on an inconspicuous spot.

Coffee on clothes

For washable fabrics, soak for half an hour in a solution of 1 teaspoon of biological liquid detergent per 2 litres of warm water. Then put into the washing machine with the hottest water that is safe for the fabric, using detergent. Resist the temptation to deal with it over the sink, by scrubbing at the stain with soap as natural soap makes tannin stains harder to remove. To remove stubborn tannin stains, you may need to wash with bleach. Try a washing booster such as Ace.

Felt-tip pen on furniture

First, try wiping the marks off with paper towels or a dry cloth. Depending on the surface, if the felt tip is still wet, you may be able to remove the mark. If not, try wiping with a clean cloth moistened with methylated spirits.

Fleas in the carpet

Vacuum all carpets, concentrating on areas frequented by your pet and under seats and sofas. Also vacuum upholstered furniture in the vicinity and then empty the vacuum bag. Wash any removable rugs or pet bedding. Using a spray bottle, apply a specialist flea killing product. The most effective are those that 'fog' the room, rather than sprays that you have to direct onto areas you suspect fleas might have moved to. Treat your pet at the same time.

Glue spills on furniture

Start by scraping up whatever you can using a dull knife. If the glue is white school glue treat it as you would a protein-based stain (page 117), which means no hot water – the hot water can cook the proteins. Spray the spot with cold water and blot with a clean cloth, repeating until clean. If it is model-making glue, blot it with a cloth dampened with dry-cleaning solvent or methylated spirits.

Lipstick on clothing

Lipstick contains both an oily/waxy base and dyes. You must first remove the oily/waxy part and then you can try to remove the dye. For washable fabrics, begin by applying a dry-cleaning solvent, such as Spotless Dry Clean Liquid. Next, rub with a liquid detergent and scrub in hot water. This should remove the oily/waxy part. Then wash in the washing machine with a detergent that contains an oxygen or all-fabric bleach.

Oil and grease on clothes

Blot up as much as you can with paper towels or carefully scrape solids up with a dull knife. For clothes that can only be dry-cleaned, blot the grease with paper towels dampened with acetone-based nail polish remover. (Don't use acetone on acetate, because it will dissolve the fabric.) For washable clothes, spray with a commercial pre-wash stain remover or use a liquid laundry detergent. Work the detergent into the stain. Immediately after pre-treatment, wash the item in your washing machine using hot water (if that is safe for the fabric and colours).

Paint on floor or carpet

Start by blotting up as much of the dripped paint as possible using paper towels. If it is latex paint, spray with clean water and blot. Repeat until you have removed as much paint as possible. If it is oil-based paint, blot with a clean cloth or paper towels moistened with paint thinner or turpentine, refreshing cloths or paper towels repeatedly. If vestiges of the paint remain on the carpet, moisten the tufts with 3 per cent hydrogen peroxide and let that stand for an hour. Blot with clean paper towels.

Pen ink stain on a pocket

Remove the pen and throw it away. Remove the item of clothing, making sure not to smear the ink stain on anything else. Place the stain face down on white paper towels. (Put plastic underneath, to keep the ink from bleeding through and staining the surface you are working on.) Wear gloves and blot with a cloth moistened with methylated spirits, forcing the stain into the paper towels. If that does not work, try white spirit. Be careful, as these solvents are flammable. Test them first in an inconspicuous corner of the material. Rinse with water and machine wash.

Mud or salt tracked in on rug

Mud wreaks havoc on a rug. Let the mud dry first and you will have a better chance of getting it out. If the mud is ground in, wait until it dries then brush it to the surface and get up as much as you can with a dull knife. After that, vacuum. If you still see muddy paw – or footprints, mix a few drops of washing-up liquid in 200ml of warm water and blot the solution onto the rug with a clean white towel. Use another damp towel to rinse and removeany remaining soap residue.

For salt stains tracked in on wet shoes and boots, mix equal parts vinegar and water and dab the mixture on with a towel. Blot with cool water and dry.

Nail polish on wooden furniture, floor or rug

Blot up the excess with a paper towel. Then blot with a cloth moistened with acetone-based nail polish remover. Don't let the nail polish remover seep into a rug's latex backing. To remove the nail polish remover, mix a solution of 1 squirt mild washing-up liquid (containing no bleach or lanolin) with 1 litre of water. Wipe the wood or work the solution into the textile with a clean towel. Draw the solution back out by blotting with a dry paper towel. Rinse by lightly spraying with clean water and then blot the water up with fresh paper towels.

Rotten smell from unknown source

Follow your nose. First, try to isolate the odour. Is it in a particular room? What do you think it might be? Is it a pet accident smell, a musty mould smell, a cooking odour? If it's in the kitchen and smells like rotten food, check the refrigerator and the bin. Look under cabinets or appliances for dropped food. If it's a musty odour, check the sink drain. Here's how to handle a few common odour problems:

• To get a horrible smell out of your kitchen bin, grind up some lemon or orange peel and drop them into it. For a more permanent fix, clean the bin thoroughly to get rid of any spilled substances.

• To keep the fridge smelling sweet, throw old food away (but seal it or take it outside, otherwise the bin will simply smell), wipe down the interior with damp paper towels and place an open box of bicarbonate of soda on a shelf inside.

Suntan lotion on clothing

Blot excess lotion with paper towels or carefully scrape the excess up with a dull knife. On washable clothes, spray the stained area with a commercial pre-wash stain remover, such as Vanish. If you do not have any, apply liquid detergent directly to the stain and work it into the stain. Immediately afterwards, machine wash in hot water (if that is safe for the fabric and colours). With dry-clean-only clothes, blot with a paper towel dampened with acetone-based nail polish remover. (Acetone will dissolve acetate, however, so don't use on that fabric.)

Water or alcohol stain on fine wood furniture

If the stain is fresh, soak up any excess water or alcohol with paper towels and then rub the spot vigorously in the direction of the grain with the palm of your hand or a cloth dipped in furniture polish. If the stain is old and dry, you will need an abrasive/lubricant combination. Apply a paste wax with a very fine grade of steel wool (such as 0000). At a pinch, you can even use cigarette ashes and mayonnaise. No matter what combination you use, rub gently in the direction of the grain using a clean, dry cloth.

Wine on the carpet

Blot up what you can with paper towels. For large spills, work from the outside in to contain the spill. Next, lightly apply a solution of ¼ teaspoon mild washing-up liquid and 2 pints of water. Work the solution into the affected area. Blot with clean paper towels to remove. Rinse by lightly spraying with water. Blot to remove excess water. Do this until all suds are gone. Then spray lightly with water and don't blot. Instead, lay a pad of paper towels down, put a weight on the pad and let the towels dry. If the stain persists,

moisten the tufts with 3 per cent hydrogen peroxide. Let it stand for an hour. Finally blot thoroughly with clean paper towels.

Wine on table linen

Regardless of the type of wine, if the fabric is washable, soak it for half an hour in a solution of 1 teaspoon of biological laundry detergent per 2 litres of warm water. Machine wash using the hottest water that's safe for the fabric. Always resist the temptation to remove wine using soap. Natural soap – including soap flakes, bar soap and detergent containing soap – makes tannin stains harder to remove. To remove stubborn tannin stains, you may need to wash the stained item with bleach.

INDEX

Acknowledgments

The following images are from the Reader's Digest Collection: 29, 30C, 37, 49, 54, 61B, 65, 109

The following images were supplied by iStockphoto.com, with the exception of 27 Elizabeth Whiting & Associates/Cole & Son Wallpaper and 88 Red Cover/Ashley Morrison

6 Baldur Tryggraston , 8-9 Elena Ray, 13 Fred Goldstein, 14 Daniel Lemay, 15 Geotrac, 16 Marc Dietrich, 17 Kirk Johnson, 18 Alex Bramwell, 19 Marilyn Nieves, 21 Johanna Goodyear, 22 Carol Gering, 23 M. Eric Honeycutt, 24 Matthew Scherf, 25 Tatiana Sayig, 26 Sean McCarthy, 28 Tammy McAllister, 30 Lorelyn Medina, 31 Dirk Diesel, 32 Kenneth C. Zirkel, 33 Michael Howard, 34 Joshua Blake, 36 Diane Diederich, 40 Stefan Klein, 41 Izabela Habur, 42 Fred Goldstein, 43 Antoski, 44 Jente Kasprowski, 45 Mark Evans, 47 Oleksandr Gumerov, 48 Adrian Moisei, 50 Roberto Adrian, 51 John Sheperd Photography, 52 Clayton Hanssen, 53 Nicholas Monu, 55 Dóri O'Connell, 56 Peter Finnie, 58 Che McPherson, 59 Dave White, 60 Kelly Cline, 61R David Ward, 62 Florida Stock, 63 Stephanie Asher, 64 Gustavo Fadel, 66 Miles Sherrill, 67 Ingvald kaldhussæter, 68 Paulo Ferrão, 69 Daniela Andreea Spyropoulos, 70 Marilyn Nieves, 71 Vlad Chiran, 72 Red Barn Studio, 73 David Parsons, 74 Perry Kroll, 75 Martin Carlsson, 76 Nocola Brown, 77 Kate Parkes, 78 Diego Cervo, 79 Serdar Yagci, 80 Kika Bisogno, 81 Joshua Blake, 82 Maurice Ciapponi, 83 Tomaz Levstek, 85 Leigh Schindler, 86 Charity Yingling, 87 Lise Gagne, 89 Amanda Rohde, 90 Phil Date, 91 Camp Spot, 92 Stan Rohrer, 93 Anne Kitzman, 94 David Freund, 95 Martina Berg, 96 Norman Pogson, 97 Sean Locke, 98 Dave Huss, 99 Pamela Moore, 100 Nancy Nehring, 102 Alden Horton, 103 Maartje van Caspel, 104R Kenneth C. Zirkel, 104B Amanda Rohde, 105 Dustin Steller, 106 Judi Ashlock, 107 Kenneth Chelette, 109 Photopix, 110 Ray Wrona, 111 Heather Nye, 112 Kate Place,113T Mark Bolton, 113B Graça Victoria, 114 Stock-IMG, 115 Amy Coldwell, 116 Jacob Wackerhausen, 117 Beat Glauser, 118 Darryl Sleath, 119T Ryan Lindberg, 119B Photolumen.com, 120 Amanda Rohde, 121 Jon Horton, 122 Nicky Gordon, 123 Scott Heiner, 124 Sharon Dominick.

Reader's Digest Household Cleaning Manual is based on material in *How to Clean Just About Anything* published by The Reader's Digest Association Limited, London

First Edition Copyright © 2007
The Reader's Digest Association Limited,
11 Westferry Circus, Canary Wharf,
London E14 4HE
www.readersdigest.co.uk

All rights reserved.
No part of this book may be reproduced, stored in a retrieval system or transmitted in any form or by any means, electronic, electrostatic, magnetic tape, mechanical, photocopying, recording or otherwise, without permission in writing from the publishers.

® Reader's Digest, The Digest and the Pegasus logo are registered trademarks of The Reader's Digest Association, Inc, of Pleasantville, New York, USA

The contents of this book are believed to be accurate at the time of printing. However the publisher accepts no responsibility or liability for any work carried out in the absence of professional advice.

We are committed to both the quality of our products and the service we provide to our customers. We value your comments, so please feel free to contact us on 08705 113366, or via our website at www.readersdigest.co.uk
If you have any comments about the content of our books, email us at gbeditorial@readersdigest.co.uk

Origination Colour Systems Limited, London
Printed and bound in China by CT Printing

READER'S DIGEST GENERAL BOOKS
Editorial Director Julian Browne
Art Director Nick Clark
Managing Editor Alastair Holmes
Head of Book Development Sarah Bloxham
Picture Resource Manager Sarah Stewart-Richardson
Pre-press Account Manager Sandra Fuller
Senior Production Controller Deborah Trott
Product Production Manager Claudette Bramble

Editor Lisa Thomas
Art Editor Julie Bennett
Proofreader Ron Pankhurst
Indexer Marie Lorimer

ISBN: 978 0 276 44209 4
BOOK CODE: 400-316 UP0000-1
ORACLE CODE: 250010678H.00.24